The Wor of War

Bruce Howard

Table of Contents

Dedication

Dedicated to my supportive parents, my beautiful wife, and my lovely children and grandchildren. May they enjoy imagining the drama of war with me.

About the Author

Bruce Howard taught science in both private and public schools for forty years, and has been the pastor of a local church for nearly thirty years. He has been married to his lovely wife Gwynne for over forty-two years and has eleven remarkable children. He is the author of "Reflections From the Quiet Corner", selections from his weekly blog.

Chapter 1: Tank

The rising summer sun's rays shimmered in the early morning light. It was already hot as Tank Hogan started hoeing the garden. His father's instructions had been clear— a little too clear—he knew he couldn't get by with anything but a long day of tending to chores. The night before Dad had peered over his bifocals with that hard, convicting gaze of his and made very sure Tank understood what was expected of him. He had to get the garden cleared of weeds, water it thoroughly, make sure the fruit trees all got their share of water, and still take care of his animals, which was his usual chore. And he would get no help either. His older brother Seth already had a summer job, and his younger siblings were all helping his mother around the house. He wondered again why his dad cared so much about planting and caring for vegetables, here where the soil was poor and the hot sun beat down mercilessly on any crops people dared to plant. Only okra and watermelon loved this kind of incessantly dry, hot weather, he thought, and they sure need the water to keep going. Of course cotton liked this kind of weather too, but fortunately his dad didn't own any fields to work, or he would certainly be out in them, keeping the weeds down. Tank was of medium but robust frame, and an excellent offensive guard on the football team, starting on the varsity squad even as a freshman, so everyone could instantly understand how he got his nickname. Clarence, his given name, didn't seem to fit him after a while, so his family and friends got to calling him Tank, because he was *"built like one."*

Living in the panhandle of Texas had its down side. It was a place he loved, but not a place where it rained very often, especially if you needed it to rain. It wasn't unusual to get two inches of rain in an hour from a thunderstorm, for it to "rain cats and dogs", and then, like turning off a faucet, the rains stopped for weeks and weeks on end. The men of the church were always asking for prayer about rain. *Why did they move to such an arid place and spend so much of their time worrying about lack of rainfall? Rain hadn't been abundant here for thousands of years.* Well, Tank didn't figure it hurt to ask for the Lord's help. He knew a lot of men who were raised without much in the way of money or things, but they relied on God to give them the strength to conquer this tough land. They were a tough people, but if it hadn't been for the windmill and the ability to pump water from the Ogallala aquifer 200 feet below the surface, nobody would live here even now. Virtually all the surface water was gyp water, full of calcium sulfate. It tasted terrible and wasn't good to drink—or use for almost anything else, for that matter. They depended on well water for everything.

There is a lot of time to think when you hoe a big garden alone. Tank's mind usually wandered to his last football game back in the fall, where they lost in the playoffs during the waning moments, or what they had been talking about in history class, his one and only favorite at school. He also couldn't help but think about his future, whether he'd ever get to leave this area of the country. It was a place he loved—he mostly loved the people he guessed—but surely there were other places to see, other things to do than work hard all the time. He'd never been over a hundred miles from his home in all his fourteen years. Oh well, nothing to be done but put your back into it and get the job done. As Dad always said, "Things don't happen by themselves; they happen because somebody uses some elbow grease to make them happen."

One thing Tank did enjoy about work, and that was the early morning time. He was perspiring already, but it wasn't going to be over a hundred degrees for a few more hours, and by then he'd be into watering and could cool off with a shower now and then. He loved listening to the meadowlarks' singing in these morning hours; they sounded so hopeful as they started their day, and their sounds were offset by the lonesome sighs of the mourning doves. Sadly there weren't a lot of trees around, hence very little shade. A few elms dotted the home place, but the fruit trees they had planted weren't very big yet. They certainly would offer no relief from the heat. He realized once more that he lived in the plains, where a man could look a long ways off and see mostly grass and sky. He wondered what it would be like to just take off walking and see what the next county or state looked like. But he was stuck here doing chores...again.

The second son of a family with four boys and two girls, he had a lot of responsibility, but he also knew how to take orders. His older brother Seth had taught him that well, and he had the old bruises to remind him of those lessons. His dad wasn't one to put up with nonsense either. Tank had experienced his share of the switch when younger, but he was smart enough to keep his mischief low key where Dad wouldn't find out...he sure hoped not, anyway. Tank didn't seem to be intimidated by much of anything, except being shut up in a tight place, that is. When he was just three his two older cousins were visiting one summer when they thought it would be a good prank to stuff him into a feed sack and tie the top down. The little boy was panic-stricken and began to scream and thrash with wild-eyed fear. The older boys, including his six-year-old brother Seth, thought it was the funniest thing they'd ever seen. Fortunately for Tank, and unfortunately for the three amigos, Tank's mother arrived at the sound of the commotion, and after releasing Tank, gave those boys a whuppin' they would remember for the rest of their lives. Tank, crying and sweating profusely, almost delirious with fear, hugged his mother for a long time, and felt insecure around Seth and the cousins for sometime thereafter. They never repeated the prank, but the damage

4

had been done. Tank had a visceral, gut-wrenching dread of dark enclosed places, and his worst nightmares involved being stuffed into those places where he slowly suffocated. It wasn't uncommon for Mother to hear his screams in the middle of the night and have to come and comfort him. More than once she lectured Seth on the foolishness of the torment they had inflicted on the little boy, and Seth felt guilty every time Tank erupted in cold sweats.

Tank forgave Seth and the cousins, and his life moved on as he grew into a strapping youngster. His one big dream was to fly, but he knew it didn't make sense. The nearest place to take lessons was Amarillo, nearly an hour and a half away; and that didn't matter anyway, because his parents couldn't afford flight lessons, and his dad was the only one who drove. At fourteen, Tank didn't have a driver's license, didn't own a car, and couldn't pay for flight lessons anyway. How could he ever learn to fly with all the obstacles in the way? He couldn't help dreaming about it though.

He was only four when Lindbergh flew solo over the Atlantic. His father had told him about it, and Dad was a good storyteller. He was able to paint a beautiful picture of what it must have been like to have that machine lift off the ground and not touch again for thirty-six hundred miles. Lindbergh didn't sleep for over fifty-five hours, but the sacrifice was worth it. He won fame for himself Tank could only try to wrap his mind around. As he swung his hoe and watered, fed his livestock and fixed fence, picked green beans and okra and corn, he dreamed. *Could he do it? Could he stay up for fifty-five hours straight? Could he learn to fly? Would he ever be seen as a hero?*

Chapter 2:Lobster Boy

Herb always thought the sea was beautiful, especially at sunrise or sunset. Others argued that the special play of colors chasing each other along the eastern or western horizons was more dazzling as the sun set on the prairie, or as it crested the Rockies at dawn, but Herb was never going to change his mind. He couldn't help but remember the words he had memorized a year or two ago:

It is a beauteous evening, calm and free,
The holy time is quiet as a Nun
Breathless with adoration; the broad sun
Is sinking down in its tranquility
The gentleness of heaven broods o'er the Sea...

Wordsworth was one of his favorite poets, and that last line about heaven brooding over the sea always felt so right to him somehow, like it had captured the essence of something important, something eternal.

Salem, Massachusetts, right on the Atlantic, was home to the Johnsons, and had been for a long time. His father had owned a whole fleet of boats of all descriptions before he had made enough money to retire to politics. Now he was a state senator and Herb enjoyed the prestige of being from an old distinguished family with enough money to afford sending him to Harvard in a couple of years. Harvard. Cambridge. Just the mention of those iconic names filled the mind with noble thoughts. How many important men had graduated from there? Lawyers, judges, ministers, scholars of all kinds. Leaders. That's what Herb wanted to be—a leader.

Herbert Vandover Johnson loved his family and three other things: lobster fishing, sailing, and books. Growing up on the water, every child in the area knew how to handle a boat, how to sail and scull. By the time he was in fourth grade Herb could take a small sailboat and make it do whatever he wanted. Yeah, Herb loved the sea and sailing more than almost anything. *Eventually maybe he would be captain of his own ship, with men to lead out on the broad ocean.*

He'd always enjoyed snorkeling for lobster too. He'd don his special gloves and take his tickle stick along, combing the rocky areas and ledges in the bay. When he noticed their antennae sticking out he'd guide the crustaceans out of their hiding spots with the stick and grab them by the carapace behind the eyes. He was good at it, too. You could use a hoop net and cat food to trap them, but for him that was too boring because he had to wait too long. Anyway, his method allowed him to toss away any undersized or oversized animals and get just the right size for boiling.

Yeah, sailing and lobster fishing. He couldn't get enough of them. Of course he loved his family too. His father and mother had been so good to him, showering him with all the kindness and grace any boy could want. He'd never needed for anything, giving him time to study the sea and books about the sea that had filled his spare hours for as long as he could remember. And he'd been given good training. "Keep in mind, Herb," Dad had always told him, "you are gifted with many blessings; use them to make a better world." His mother, a beautiful dark-haired daughter of the Vandover clan, was equally insistent that Herb devote himself to becoming the kind of man that would make them proud. She loved books, especially books of poetry, and she had made Herb love poetry too. She had a special way of reading a poem that was a beautiful thing in itself. Through reading to him she had touched him until words resonated and became a part of him. He had memorized at his mother's insistence the Henry Vaughan poem *The Retreat...*

Happy those early days! When I shined in my angel infancy.
Before I understood this place appointed for my second race,
Or taught my soul to fancy aught but a white, celestial thought;
When yet I had not walked above a mile or two from my first love,
And looking back, at that short space, could see a glimpse of His bright face;
When on some gilded cloud or flower my gazing soul would dwell an hour,
And in those weaker glories spy some shadows of eternity...

A love of poetic language knit Herb to his mother in a special way. Both of them could somehow see a shadow of eternity in those words, and Herb resolved that he would see to it that he fulfilled his parents' hopes for him.

At fifteen years of age Herb was already just a touch over six feet tall, and looked the part of a young captain at the helm of his sailboat. Well-proportioned and handsome, girls had been noticing Herbert Johnson for months now. He had just the right mixture of fun and sobriety in his personality. He could talk about world history with the adults, quote poetry from memory, and the next minute be doing the Dipsey Doodle as Tommy Dorsey played in the background. All the girls in high school knew Herb was what they called *"a keeper."* He might be a tad young yet, but he was worth keeping an eye on. A gentleman and a scholar. One day a Harvard graduate and leader of men. He was destined to go far.

Another of the poems that was one of his mother's favorites was Longfellow's poem about life and our duty to live it to the full for the glory of God. He didn't have it all down yet, but he was working on committing it to memory…

Tell me not in mournful numbers, life is but an empty dream!
For the soul is dead that slumbers, and things are not what they seem.

Life is real! Life is earnest! And the grave is not its goal;

Dust thou art, to dust returnest, was not spoken of the soul.

Not enjoyment, and not sorrow, is our destined end or way;
But to act that each tomorrow, find us farther than today.

Art is long, and Time is fleeting, and our hearts though
stout and brave,
Still, like muffled drums are beating funeral marches to the
grave.

In the world's broad field of battle, in the bivouac of Life,
Be not like dumb, driven cattle! Be a hero in the strife!

Trust no Future, howe'er pleasant! Let the dead Past bury
its dead;
Act—act in the living Present! Heart within and God
o'erhead!

Lives of great men all remind us, we can make our lives
sublime,
And departing, leave behind us, footprints on the sands of
time.

Footprints, that perhaps another, sailing o'er life's solemn
main,
A forlorn and shipwrecked brother, seeing, shall take heart
again.

Let us, then, be up and doing, with a heart for any fate;
Still achieving, still pursuing, learn to labor and to wait.

That line near the end, about making life sublime and
leaving footprints on the sands of time...*that* is what Herbert
Vandover Johnson wanted his life to be!

Chapter 3: Big Sky

Montana has been called Big Sky Country since at least eighteen eighty-nine, when it became the forty-first state. In the eastern part of the state this makes sense, because rolling grassy hills undulate unendingly to the horizon. It was where Custer perished at the Little Bighorn. In that part of Montana, as in all plains states, you can see miles and miles of more miles and miles. But the western third of the state is true mountain country. The Northern Rocky Mountains and a hundred smaller ranges block the skyline in this rugged terrain, and there are times the snow or rain on the western slopes blocks out the sky altogether. Of course, that would be a lot more snowfall than rainfall; less than half the U.S. average rainfall, but nearly twice the average U.S. snowfall.

Kit Anderson loved the place. He was born near the Idaho border four miles northwest of Missoula to a father and mother who could take care of themselves and the seven children born to them. They were a proud, self-reliant people. Kit's kin came from pure pioneer stock, and they were as independent and strong as people could possibly be. They hunted for their meat, cured it themselves, and still traded furs for many of their other necessities. Kit had a lot in common with his namesake, iconic frontiersman Kit Carson, including small size, a strong yet gentle personality until riled, and being "clean as a hound's tooth." One of

Carson's acquaintances described him that way, and it expressed everyone's assessment of Kit Anderson as well. From his earliest days he was a guy you could trust. Competent, unassuming, and willing to pull his weight were terms people used when letting others know what they thought of him.

His dad taught him to hunt, trap, and fish from childhood, and he loved to be outdoors, just like all his friends. He was highly intelligent, but not necessarily with book learning. While attending class in his small school his mind wandered into the mountains instead of focusing on English or Math lessons. He completed his assignments on time—his father wouldn't put up with tardiness in any form—but his heart wasn't really in his schoolwork. Each day found him anxious for the last bell to ring so he could hurry home, finish his chores, and set off to check his traps or fish for trout in one of the many clear mountain streams near his home. One thing he never forgot to take on these trips was his gun. Dad had taught him well on that point. "Never go out without it," he had said. "Too many bear and cougar and wolves in these mountains, and they ain't always friendly you know."

Kit shot his first elk at age eight, his first cougar at age twelve. He knew how to field dress an elk, had heard and believed the old saying that "elk hunting ceases to be fun the moment you pull the trigger," but he enjoyed the camaraderie working with a couple of men as they positioned the bull or cow elk so that it wouldn't roll, then separated from each other a bit so one could work on the hind quarter, one on the front quarter, while the third caped the bull if it was to have its head mounted on somebody's wall at home.

Kit learned that it was a myth to have to slit the animals' throat to bleed it out—once the heart stops the bleeding stops. And the animal didn't need to be gutted either. They could get plenty of meat without disemboweling the game. It didn't take long to realize that bone was heavy, so the meat needed to be cut off the bone. Backstrap is removed from the carcass, then tenderloins. He learned to keep the meat clean, away from hair and the ground, and then of course it had to be divvied up so that each person carried roughly the same amount out. It was plenty of work for sure!

But Kit relished the times spent with these mountain men, men who were so self-sufficient and capable. They had their own kind of discipline, their own set of ways that they had learned from their fathers, who had learned from their fathers before them. Despite his size, Kit proved he belonged among them, part of a rare fellowship of rugged mountain men.

Because of his small size, Kit was the target of each new bully that came to his school; but the bullying never lasted very long. He remembered the first, Joey Thomas, the kid who had moved up from Pinesdale and wanted to throw his weight around the tiny school because he thought he was tougher than anybody there. Kit was in the second grade, and Joey in the fourth. Joey almost immediately made an impact on his new school, and nearly all the impact was bad. He'd pushed younger kids around and made life miserable for all of them, especially Kit. Kit had gone home and complained to his folks, and his dad had drawn him aside and given him some advice. "Bullies have always been a part of school, son. And there's one thing I know about them. They won't stop bullying because you complain to the adults. They only stop when somebody stops them. You can't let him push you around, or it will never end. I know he's bigger and stronger, but because he's a bully I also know he's a coward. You take the lead and teach him a lesson he won't forget, and you'll be the hero of your class." The very next day Kit took his father's advice. When Joey picked on some third grade girls at recess Kit came up and told him to stop. Joey sneered and said, "And I suppose *you* are gonna stop me?!" With that, the fight was on. When the teacher finally found out about the ruckus, Joey had an eye that was going to be black the next day and Kit was bleeding from his mouth and nose, but seemed ready for more. He was ready to blacken Joey's other eye, and seriously rearrange his facial features to boot.

Kit's dad was proud of his son for standing up to the threat, but knew he needed more training to learn to take care of himself, so he enrolled Kit in a boxing class. Kit learned quickly that size wasn't the biggest factor in a fight, that quick reflexes and skill could more than make up for a weight or height disadvantage. Kit seemed to instinctively understand leverage, and how to get another to commit to a punch and end up off balance and open to a counterpunch. By the time he was fifteen he had won several area bantamweight boxing titles, and nearly all of the bullying had come to a screeching halt. Kit Anderson, like the old Kit Carson, was a man to be underestimated at another's own risk.

Chapter 4: Training a Tank to Fly

High school Graduation Day, nineteen forty-two. Tank could hardly believe the day was here. Like most teen boys he had been pulling at the reins harder and harder as the years went by, feeling he was ready to leave home and make it on his own, and he knew he was fixing to bust if he didn't get on with his life. He had learned so much working at Hill's Garage the last two years, finally felt that he was a decent mechanic who could rebuild a carburetor or diagnose and repair an engine problem instead of just staring stupidly under the hood like most of his friends. And now he was ready to go to Pre-Midshipman School, staying in Texas for now, but farther from home than he'd ever been, with the ultimate goal of heading to North Carolina and Naval Aviation training.

Tank had signed up weeks ago. His father said he was proud; his mother cried some tears and said she feared she was losing another of her boys. But his older brother Seth had joined the Army infantry, was already trained up and shipping out soon for Germany, and he certainly wasn't going to let Seth get all the glory. Seth would always be stuck on the ground while he was going to be a flier, where you could really have the adventures, and be farther from the bullets! To soar as Lindbergh had! Could anything be better?!

Pre-Midshipman School was a lot of work, three months of intensive basic flight training in an N3N biplane trainer; followed by fourteen more weeks of intermediate training. But Tank took to flying like a fish takes to water. Now that he had a reason to learn math—it made more sense to him when applied to airplanes and flight—he studied as much as time allowed. He didn't want to fail; he *would not* fail at fulfilling this lifelong dream. The country was paying for his training, and he was not about to lose out on this chance at being a flyboy. From the panhandle plains of Texas to the wild blue yonder. God was answering his prayers.

Chapel Hill, North Carolina! That was the next stop, to enroll in the Navy's AVCAD (Aviation Cadet) program. You had to be unmarried, between eighteen and twenty-six, and have completed either two years of college or the Pre-Midshipman School, and Tank fit the bill in every way. You also had to be in top physical condition, and intelligent. Tank knew he wasn't the greatest of classroom students, except in history, and increasingly in math, but he understood machines and except for flying he loved nothing better than greasy hands and the smell of gasoline and the shop. Tank had heard the washout rate in the training program was fairly high, but he had also heard that pilots were needed desperately, so he hoped that gave him a leg up. All he wanted was an opportunity to show what he could do.

Tests, tests, and more tests! Tank was sick of them. There were psychological tests, psychomotor tests, physical fitness and coordination tests. Thankfully he scored very high on the tests for hand-eye-foot coordination; that marked him out as a prime candidate for being a pilot. You also got into the air if you were a bombardier or gunner or navigator, but what he really wanted was to be the guy on the stick, with the big plane under his control. It reminded him of two kinds of guys he knew: guys who just enjoyed the car ride and those that had to drive. He was a driver, no doubt about it, even if now instead of a car it was a Stearman biplane, everyone's training craft.

But for now he was just one of the grunts. Up at five a.m. every morning, running through rivers that came up to your chin, hiking up and down stairs with a backpack full of sand strapped to your back. Tank was in the best shape of his life, but he was so tired at the end of each day that he could hardly move. He expended so much energy that he was ravenously hungry, and that was the one saving grace of the training— they fed you thousands of calories a day. He and his buddies would need every ounce of that energy, because it was six hours a day of physically difficult training for three intense months, and not all the fatigue was from the physical exertion. There were still classes, classes, and more classes to attend and mountains of information to absorb. Tank went from excellent to superb physical condition, and took great pride in his academic work ethic in training school as well. He wanted to learn everything he could that would make him a better flyer. He knew his survival might one day depend on some skill he was learning now.

One night John Collins, Fred Dixon, and Tank were getting ready to hit the rack when Collins asked, "Hey Tank, did you read the manual the old man wrote about our little paradise here?"

Tank had read it. "Yeah, said we came from a 'soft, luxurious, loose-thinking, lazy peacetime home.' He never had my dad to work for. Soft was getting up with the chickens, and luxurious was hoeing and watering and feeding livestock and fixing tractors all day."

"He said our enemies had been trained since they were kids to wage war. Think that's true?"

"Sure could be. I never been to Japan or Germany. But those that have been raised hardscrabble like you and me will hold our own, I reckon."

Dixon chimed in, "Hey, did you hear we got another one of those fourteen-mile hikes through the jungle tomorrow night? Colonel says we gotta be able to fend for ourselves if we crash land on an island."

"That fourteen-mile hike can take a hike. Remember how hard it was last time? The base mascot Colonel Brown couldn't even handle it. You know it's tough when the camp dog can't even survive. I couldn't believe it did him in and we made it. But there's one type of training I really enjoy, when they drop you somewhere and you got to use survival skills to be able to get water, find the right berries to eat, make and use a fish hook and line, and navigate by the stars. You even have to know how to handle venomous snakes. If I didn't want to fly so bad I sometimes think it'd be fun just to be a commando for awhile, sneak out of camp and play hide-and-seek out there in the jungle, make 'em come and find us. Course the bad thing about it would be they'd probably court-martial us for sneaking out once they found us."

One thing Tank didn't like at all was the mandatory sports drills every afternoon. Guys were encouraged to not play by the rules, and this always led to lots of scrapes between the men. In basketball there were never any fouls called, and so guys just hacked and pushed and bloodied each others' noses at will. Same thing in the soccer matches. You sure learned to keep your eyes out for opponents sneaking up on you. Jump to head a ball and get kicked who knows where while you're up there. It was dog-eat-dog, alright. Tank just figured that their leaders were trying to remind them daily that the Japs were going to try and kill or abuse them in the worst ways possible, and they might as well get used to it. The idea was, if you got knocked down, you just kept on getting back up.

21

Tank did enjoy the pushball and aerowheel games. The pushball was huge, and there were twelve men on each team. The object was simple; push the ball past the opponents and over their goal line. Tank wasn't that tall, but very powerful, and had lots of stamina. He was perfect for the game, and he enjoyed the teamwork necessary to win the contest. The aerowheel was a fun device that you strapped your feet into and rolled around in to improve balance, coordination, and core strength. It was certainly a challenge.

The swimming was the toughest part for Tank, and he found out quickly that he wasn't the only one who didn't have a lot of aquatic skills. Raised in the panhandle of Texas, water sports weren't something he had done a lot. But when you fly thousands of miles over open water, and they were certainly going to do that, you had to be able not only to land on water but be able to swim if you had to. Tank was in the greatest shape of his life, but the mile swim just about did him in every time. He just couldn't seem to get the hang of swimming effortlessly like Collins and Borden. They had swum in competitions in high school, were long and had huge feet that made good flippers. Tank just wondered if he could dog paddle long enough to stay afloat until someone found him. And he desperately hoped the one who found him wasn't going to be a shark.

They also had the boys dive to a depth of fifty feet, but Tank never understood the rationale behind that one. Heck, anybody could sink to that depth, as long as they weren't required to come up again. Were they practicing for pearl diving or so they could treasure hunt under the water?

"Hey, Tank, did you hear what we gotta practice tomorrow?" asked Borden one day.

"No, what is it they've got for us now?"

"They're going to make us dive into pools that have oil floating on the water, oil they've lit on fire."

"No way, what are they tryin' to do, make fried chicken of us?"

"No, they say that if you're on a ship that gets torpedoed oil fires are one of the most dangerous things you can face. I guess they want us to practice how to dive in and swim under the fire."

"But what if the fire is too big to dive and swim under? Did they ever think of that? Look, I don't need practice diving under fire water, because I don't ever intend to be on a ship that gets torpedoed. That's why I'm in the air force."

"Right. Well, things don't always go as planned, do they? Oh, they also want us to practice getting out of a submerged cockpit, in case we ever have to do that."

Tank had heard about this one. "Yeah, I knew that was coming. I also heard that a cadet named Needham drowned the last time they had that training a few weeks back. Stuff like that sure makes you excited to try the new drills they have for us, doesn't it?"

Dixon added, "Well Tank, it doesn't make any difference whether we're excited or not. I guess they didn't ask us what we thought about the training."

Tank just sighed. *True enough*, he thought.

Fred Dixon and Tank had hit it off from the start. Dixon was from Oklahoma, so they told all the Okie/Texas jokes they knew, and teased each other about what group was smarter, and whether the University of Oklahoma or the University of Texas had the better football team, but they were raised in similar homes, where work ethic and Christian faith were bedrocks of existence, and they both spoke the same Southern country language. John Collins was also one of Tank's favorites. Sensible, calm, and intelligent, he was the kind of man that just didn't have many enemies.

Training was alternately the most grueling, difficult, demanding, and yet boring, most tedious thing any of them had ever done. Like all men of war since the beginning everyone's favorite pastime was to gripe. In fact, it seemed in some ways almost all anyone ever did was gripe; about the weather, about the food, about their jobs, about the drills, about everything. But Tank figured everything had a reason, and he was determined to give it all his best.

They did have a little time to engage in some traditional sports like baseball, and Tank always enjoyed that. Fred was a great shortstop, and Tank had been a good little leaguer, with a good eye for the ball. But he wasn't quite good enough to make the base team, the one that actually got to play teams from other outfits. He had never met the guy, but he heard the base team had a fellow named Ted Williams that had played a couple of years in the majors with the Red Sox, and who could hit anything anybody could throw at him.

Another thing Tank enjoyed was marksmanship. He hadn't done a lot of hunting, but guns were machines, and machines he understood. One part of him thought *"Hey, I'm the pilot. What do I need to be able to shoot for?"* But then he realized you never knew what kind of jam you were going to get into, and then being able to use that gun might be pretty handy.

Besides the grinding physical demands, the school was, after all, a school, so Tank had classes in Morse code, navigation, meteorology, seamanship, physics, and even psychology. At first the seamanship part of the course was a pain, because Tank wanted to fly, not handle a boat; but when you were going to be flying over water, those skills could sure come in handy if you needed them. Brass estimated that eighty percent of them would be in the water before the war was over. Tank, of course, sure hoped it never came to that. Just the thought of paddling around with sharks gave him the cold shivers.

The instructor also told them that if they were captured, they would need all the psychological skills they could get. Tank was going to do everything possible to insure that he never got captured to see if he needed those skills. Oh, and one more thing in their training: they learned how to kill a man twelve different ways with their bare hands. Tank hoped all the enemy he killed he never saw because he'd be thousands of feet above their heads when the bombs detonated.

"We sure don't have a lot of free time for socializing, do we?" asked Collins one day at chow.

"What did you think, they brought us here to turn us into frat boys?"

"Well, at least we get Wednesday afternoons, Saturday afternoons and nights, and Sunday afternoons to do what we want."

"Yeah, sure glad we have some time to write home or just get away and relax a bit. Those times it feels like I'm livin' in high cotton."

Collins told Tank and Dixon they sure had some funny phrases they used. Collins was from Pennsylvania where he didn't hear those kinds of things.

"I'll give you the best phrase of all," Tank said, "It's a Southern phrase you can use and get away with anything while you are griping or saying something not so complimentary about somebody."

"What is it, a magic phrase?" Collins was genuinely interested.

"Almost. Just say 'bless their heart.'" Tank was grinning.

"Bless their heart? What does that even mean?"

Tank smiled even bigger. "Well, you can use it this way...'that cook is the lousiest I've ever seen, bless his heart.' Or you could say 'those drill sergeants and flight instructors are the dumbest, meanest, sorriest cusses this side of the grave, bless their hearts.' Or you even might try, 'She's the ugliest girl I ever saw, bless her heart.' You can say anything about anybody, as long as you add that phrase at the end."

Collins only had one thing to say to the Texan and the Okie: "I'll never understand you Southerners, bless your hearts."

Chapter 5: A Sky-High Tank

Flight training was incredibly intense during those days. The number of pilots and crews needed to wage a two-front war taxed the ability of the United States to keep 'em coming; especially since those planes, pilots and crews were being lost at an alarming rate.

The pilot's job description was more than lengthy. On a big bomber there were more than twenty-five gauges on the panel, different levers for the throttle, turbocharger, and fuel mixture, and there were over a dozen switches. Then there was fighting the wheel. It wasn't too bad on a B-17, but for a B-24 it was like driving a large truck with no power steering.

And the pilot didn't just have to understand all the contraptions needed to keep the plane in the air. He needed to understand each crew member's job thoroughly as well, and be able to perform their duties in case of emergency. There was a lot to know. Bomb crews were composed of gunners, engineers, navigators, bombers, and radiomen, as well as the pilot and co-pilot, and each member of the crew was proficient in their craft...or so everyone hoped. The pilot had a lot to learn, and he had to learn it fast. Pilots and planes were being lost at such a rate that the officers sped up training, and then began to cut it short so they could bring new men into the line.

Fortunately Ray McAllen was the best flight instructor Tank had ever seen. "Smooth as glass," Tank said of him later. Ray told him, "Don't think this is going to be easy, because it's not. Your job will be to handle this plane so well that you and everybody on it gets home from every mission. *My* job is to make sure that you are eminently qualified to do *your* job." Ray taught Tank how to read all those gauges, use all those switches, how to manipulate the flaps, use the rudders, keep the plane level, take off and land. If Tank made a mistake or hesitated, Ray gave him fits. But when it was all over, Tank felt he could fly anything anywhere and get back safely again.

One evening Ray was teaching Tank about night flying in the B-17, using his compass to find his way. They were nearly a hundred miles from base when Ray leaned back in his seat and said, "Take us home." It was dark as pitch, with no lights below to help in orientation, and no navigator along. Tank wondered if he could do it. It didn't help when Ray added, "If you can't get us back to base I'm going to recommend that they wash you out. I can't send men up with you if you can't get them back home again."

Tank began to sweat cold bullets, but told himself this is what he had dreamed about for years, what he was in training for, and he sure wasn't going to mess it up now if he could help it. Finally getting his mind back in gear, Tank thought about all the lessons Ray had drilled into him, and then it clicked. He regained his composure, and within minutes the plane was oriented correctly, and the journey home began. Seeing the base runway and landing that plane had never felt sweeter to him.

It was a good thing Tank had gotten through Ray McAllen's training, because McAllen wasn't doing the final test for earning his wings. Up to now, as hard as it had been, it had all been fun and games. Tank couldn't help but think *it's do or die time when my approval flight test comes up.*

Early in their training they had been issued a sheet that asked their preferences for the planes they would be trained to fly: fighter planes, two-engine short-range bombers, or four-engine long-range bombers. They needed pilots for long-range bombers, because fewer guys wanted to fly those, but Tank thought those planes were just right for him. The fighter guys were the glory boys who enjoyed being lone wolves on the prowl and catching the headlines in the newspapers, but those bombers were every bit as instrumental to winning a war as the fighter planes were, and the bomber pilots not only had their own skin to worry about, but the lives of every man on their crew. It wasn't a job for cowards. Tank had always been responsible—for his chores, for his younger brothers and sisters, for the younger kids on his football team who needed encouragement. Now he was responsible for the lives of every man on board an airplane.

It took a special kind of guy to embrace that kind of duty, but Tank believed he was that special kind of guy.

Tank couldn't help feeling sorry for the guys who washed out. Flight Instructor John Sanders was as sharp as they come, knew flying inside and out, but was the toughest guy Tank had ever met, and his standards for his pilots were high. Seems he washed out a guy or two a day. Tank really missed Hubbard and Dixon. They had both been flushed last week, and Tank had seen Dixon cry because he wanted to fly so badly. Maybe they could circle back in their training and become bombardiers or gunners or navigators. Tank heard that some of the guys who were rejected as pilots just got transferred to the infantry, and he knew his friends dreaded that with a passion.

Flight Instructor Leon Atkins had a reputation as one who might go a bit easier on you in your approval flight, but Tank wanted to be approved by the best, and he hoped when the time came he could stand up to Sanders' scrutiny. He hated the idea of moving on in his career with some of his buddies ribbing him about getting there the easy way.

Tank's day came, and sure enough, Sanders was tagged as the man to certify him, but he had some time to kill before Sanders was ready, so he decided to take the trainer plane up and get the butterflies out of his system. Flying alone seemed to always calm him down. It had rained hard the night before, and on landing Tank came in a bit hot, wanting to make sure he cleared the barbed wire fence. He hit the water which covered part of the field, which caused the plane's nose to dip and the tail to rise. He jumped out of the machine and pulled the tail down, hoping nobody had seen the mishap.

But wouldn't you know it—here came Sanders, face a frozen scowl. "Ready to go up, Hogan?"

Tank knew Sanders had seen the landing which he had blown, and that his performance in this test flight had better be flawless, because Sanders was just looking for a reason to knock him off the pilots' list. *Well, what have I got to lose? I'm going to let go and give this officer the ride of his life.* For some strange reason that idea calmed him and lightened his mood, and he had his best day of flying yet. He kept remembering Ray McAllen's advice, "Don't let the aircraft fly you; you fly it." Tank got in the zone and did every task impeccably, from sharp turns to slow easy turns to simulated engine failure protocols to pulling out of a dive. And every question about the rudder, the ailerons and flaps, the gauges, everything Sanders could throw at him Tank answered quickly and precisely.

His landing was perfect this time, and Sanders shook his head. "All I can say is you're lucky Hogan. When I got in this plane I had every intention of flunking you out, but you've got what it takes. You're approved."

Tank's buddies couldn't believe it. Collins said, "Here you almost wrecked a plane, right in front of the toughest FI at the base, and you still passed!"

"Yeah, I can't believe Sanders checked me through. He's the hardest teacher I've ever had."

"Hey, you ought to be a Japanese trainee. I read about their routines. They do something wrong they get hit with a baseball bat!" Collins still couldn't believe what he had just read.

"Come on, that can't be right." Tank wasn't buying the idea at all. It seemed too preposterous to contemplate.

"It *is* right. They get hit if they don't land right or drink too much sake, or do anything else the instructors don't like. The article said the instructor sits behind them in the training plane and cracks them over the head while they're flying if they mess up. And one more thing: everybody in a unit gets banged around if one person flops. I guess they're trying to improve *esprit de corps*!"

"Listen goofball, if I was getting banged around with a baseball bat because of your screw-ups, it wouldn't help my *esprit de corps* one little bit!"

But Tank was ecstatic. He was going to be a pilot! The way he felt today, he almost wouldn't mind getting hit with a bat—almost.

Graduating high school wasn't that big a deal to him, just an event that followed many years of boring schoolwork. But graduating from flight academy! That was different. He had on his dress uniform, his beautiful hat, and today he would have his gold Navy Aviator wings pinned on. First Lieutenant Clarence Potter Hogan. The photographer was taking the official pictures, and he couldn't wait to get a copy to send back home. How envious his younger brothers would be, how proud his mom and dad, and how the old high school girls would swoon!

Chapter 6: Leaving Harvard

Herb was confused. He had grown up with books, loved reading them, memorizing poetry, studying the classics, and preparing to fulfill his one great dream: entrance into the elite world of Harvard University. It had been the guiding vision throughout his early childhood and teen years. Established in sixteen thirty-six and named after clergyman and benefactor John Harvard, it was the oldest and most prestigious university in America, allowing only one in twenty applicants to enter and pursue a degree there. It was the elite of the elite, and it was a place Herbert Vandover Johnson felt he belonged. Harvard's coat of arms contained the Latin word *veritas*, meaning truth, and Herb was dedicated to pursuing that wherever it led. Crimson was Harvard's color, and Herb couldn't wait to wear it with pride.

He had been accepted; that in itself was quite an honor. Yet after only a year of study, a very successful year where he made the Deans' Honor Roll, he felt so strongly about the war as he began his second year that he knew he must withdraw from school and join up. He had seen handbills announcing war bond suppers and drives to support the war, and he just couldn't sit still while the rest of the country did their part to help. Herb had been growing more anxious by the month, because Karl Doenitz, head of German U-boats, was sending more and more of them into American waters to threaten American merchant marines. To Herb this was personal because he knew so many of these men by name and respected their service to their country. German U-boat attacks had begun in January along the Eastern Seaboard, sinking fuel tankers and cargo ships with impunity and often within sight of the shore. In less than seven months these attacks had sunk two hundred thirty-three ships in the Atlantic Ocean and Gulf of Mexico and killed over five thousand seamen and passengers, more than twice the number of victims at Pearl Harbor. Herb knew some of the victims and their families well, and he couldn't get it out of his mind. He couldn't study with clarity.

At least with his love for sailing the part of his decision about which area of service to join was easy. Here it was, October third, nineteen forty-two, and he was being sworn into the U.S. Navy service with one hundred twenty-four other men in the Salem courthouse by Lieutenant Harvey Jones. He had packed his duffel bag, and was ready for the great adventure.

His father understood his feelings, the tug-of-war in his soul over continuing school or joining up to fight for his country. His mother was a different story. For the life of her she couldn't appreciate or accept his conviction that he could not stand idly by while his country went to war. "But you can help the cause in other ways, as an engineer or doctor or professor," was her way of putting it. How hard it had been to go against her wishes. She had always been so kind to him, so gentle. The thought of breaking her heart tormented him.

But he couldn't change how he felt, and he couldn't dwell on his mother's fears and anxieties; there was too much else to occupy his mind. The bus left for the airport and his flight across the country in just a few more hours. He needed to say goodbye one last time to the folks, and then to Karen. He and Karen had dated steadily the last two years of high school, and he had left her to go to college, twice, and now would have to leave her again. He couldn't help but wonder if she would wait for him to return so they could get on with their lives together some day. He rushed from the courthouse and found Karen on break from her job at the drugstore. Herb was a young man who didn't like drama, who preferred application of cool analysis to problems so that effective solutions could be found quickly. A woman and her emotions was a much harder path for him to navigate. But there was no escaping the drama with his mother, and now with Karen too.

At first it seemed she didn't want to see him. She was so teary that she didn't think she could handle the goodbye; but she knew they had to spend a bit more time together, before…who knew what. She stood quietly with her arms around his waist, hands tightly clasped behind his back, her head cradled in the curve of his cheek while her tears fell onto his jacket. Herb, usually so full of beautiful and appropriate words, tried to speak reassuringly, but found it impossible to find anything that sounded right for the circumstance. He had memorized a poem to share with her, but as he tried to speak it his voice caught and wouldn't function. Thankfully he had written it down, and finally pulling away and uttering a husky "goodbye", he kissed her, and left her the poem, the English translation of the Hawaiian *Aloha* song:

Farewell to thee, farewell to thee

Thou charming one who dwells in shaded bowers

One fond embrace ere I depart

Until we meet again.

He hoped and prayed that God *would* hold her safe until they could meet again…and he hoped and prayed the same for himself. He was very much aware that he was entering the time of greatest uncertainty in his young life. Where would he end up? What would it be like to man the guns of a great warship and launch thousands of rounds of ordnance against the Germans or the Japanese? As intelligent as he was, he couldn't begin to see the answers to those questions, and it distressed him.

He couldn't help but think now about John McRae's somber poem from World War I:

In Flanders fields the poppies grow amid the crosses, row on row

That mark our place, and in the sky, the larks, still bravely singing, fly

We are the dead. Short days ago, we lived, saw sunset glow

Loved, and were loved, and now we lie in Flanders fields

Loved, and were loved! Herb had known the love of a dear father and mother, and the budding love of a sweetheart, and he certainly returned those loves. He wondered if he would ever return home alive to those dear ones who had captured his heart.

Chapter 7: Herb Joins Up

After taking the oath to join the U.S. Navy, Herb thought his next stop would be Newport, Rhode Island, and the naval training base there. It was the oldest of the four stations then in use by the navy for training, and it was the one closest to home. It wouldn't be too far to travel to see the folks or Karen when he got leave. Norfolk, Virginia, also had a base, the country's largest at the time, and it wasn't too far away either, only eleven hours away. But Herb was to learn the military truism that "once you join up, they *own you*." As badly as sailors were needed in the Atlantic for the European war with Germany and Italy, they were needed even more in the Pacific in the fight against the Japanese. The Pacific war had started out as a flop, no matter what the pro-American propaganda said, and something had to change. So it was a long flight to San Diego, California for Herb and the others from the Northeast who had enlisted. Liberty Station, here we come! And Herb thought ruefully, *I couldn't be farther from home.*

The recruits arrived and gathered in Luce Auditorium, which had just been completed. The orientation was brief, and then they got moving. Like all the recruits, entering Boot Camp for Herb was a whirlwind of activity. Shots, a buzz haircut, discarding all his possessions to receive new clothes by the Navy Supply Clerks, then moving down the line like a part of an assembly plant, picking up the bits and pieces of equipment that would be part of his new life—it was all a big blur. And in the navy as opposed to the other branches of service you even received and carried your bed, a hammock with a mattress, pillow, and two blankets. The guy behind Herb, George Keller, asked him where in the world they were supposed to store all the goodies. It didn't take long to find out, because at the end of the line each man was issued a sea bag. It had grommets at the top so the man could weave a line through them and make a draw string.

As with everything else he got, Herb was instructed to stencil his name on the side so his new possessions weren't mixed up with the other men's. The labeled contents of his bag gave him his only unique identity as an individual among the mass of other trainees. Everything about the place was designed to teach men to be part of a team. Even the calisthenics and drills had to be repeated if someone lagged behind or got out of cadence. Team, team, team; everyone depending on everyone else to pull their weight.

Herb slung the bag onto his shoulder and marched off with all he now owned on his back, but only after he had loaded the bag according to instructions. Herb heard murmurs of complaint from those nearest him about the "persnickety rules," but he found out nothing was arbitrary in those orders. Without carefully rolling clothing to take up a minimum of space in the bag, and then rolling the bedding

41

correctly, a man couldn't get everything into it that was necessary. Herb thought, *at least this regulation makes sense and is practical.*

Last of all Herb was issued the navy's bible, *The Bluejackets' Manual.* It had all the information he needed to become a sailor. After finding his barracks and stowing his gear in his locker, he reported for roll call and his first bit of naval wisdom.

"I'm Chief Petty Officer Adams, and I am your principal instructor during your seven weeks here. I want to remind you that I am not your mommy, and I will not be *asking* you to follow the rules and do your best. I am your superior officer and I am *telling you* what you will do and how you will do it. You *will* do your best at all times. Learn to obey orders promptly and vigorously. If you do you will stand the best chance of surviving this war and returning to those who will take it easier on you."

The first five days of boot camp were called P-days, or processing days. By that time everyone had gotten the hang of life around camp, the rigors and the pranks from other enlistees. Herb had met a couple of Southern boys, Ollie Hill and Virgil Ballard, and they had hit it off immediately. Ollie was from Alabama and Virgil from Oklahoma. Funny how moving three thousand miles from home made you open up to people who couldn't be more different from you. Herb, a brilliant Harvard scholar from a prominent family in the Northeast, now had great friends from lower middle income American families in the South. The three guys spent almost every available minute together when they had breaks, which didn't seem very often. The military understood that the more time young men had to goof off, the goofier things they would think of to do.

Herb couldn't believe it. After enduring the hardest day yet, ten hours of marching, calisthenics, scrubbing clothes, rifle-over-your head drills with his ten-pound Garand M1 rifle, pulling oars, and loading heavy shells into the five-inch gun, now he was awakened in the middle of the morning by the CPO shouting obscenities and waking everyone up for inspection. Later Herb realized the navy was just trying to get them accustomed to discipline, to respond quickly and quietly to disagreeable orders, to function promptly with little sleep—and probably to give Adams his little kicks as he showed his absolute control over them. But whatever it took to become a sailor, he was all in. Adams was especially particular about the care and use of their rifle. "You'll need to get so used to this weapon that it becomes just another part of your body." Adams taught them how to run with it, how to jump over obstacles with it, how to spring up with it in advance, and how to fall down with it so that you didn't damage it. Adams told them that the M1 could kill three men, passing through the first two until it lodged in the third.

43

After firing it Herb believed him. It was a fantastic weapon. Virgil found out that George Patton, famous here in San Diego even though he was on the other side of the world fighting Germans at the moment, had declared it "the greatest battle implement ever devised." Herb was fascinated to learn later that the navy had actually studied high-speed pictures to improve the training. Adams repeated it over and over again, and Herb came to believe it: "Remember boot, everything, and I mean *everything* we teach you, has a reason."

As the training progressed, the difficulties of the tasks increased. It was especially hard to climb horizontal ropes with full packs, rifles, helmets, bayonets, and plenty of extra ammo clips, but *this is the type of thing we might be asked to do*, thought Herb. *Everything we teach you has a reason.* Even the hand-to-hand combat practice. It was a bit hard for Herb to wrap his mind around desperate face-to-face battle for survival with another human being. He sort of imagined that he'd be loading shells into guns and preparing depth charges for blasting enemy submarines rather than fighting for his life in some jungle. *But you never knew what to expect, did you?*

Herb had no problem with the rigorous discipline, the physical training, or the material to memorize and the class-work. Ollie and Virgil, his two best friends, were intimidated in the classroom. "You've got to help us, Herb," Ollie confided one day after evening mess. "I never was much good in school, and I just can't seem to get the hang of all these facts and calculations."

"Ollie, I'll be glad to help you and Virgil anyway I can. Implausible as it may sound, the Lord has given me ample brainpower to determine the correct course of action here and instruct you both in the vagaries of naval science, provided you are both willing to hit your studies wholeheartedly and with robustness."

Virgil gave Ollie a quizzical look and said, "We'll be glad to serve under you sir, just as long as you tone down them words a bit so we can understand more of them."

Herb was good-hearted and enjoyed immensely helping out Ollie and Virgil. They spent any spare moments they could find in the week poring over the lessons. Ollie hadn't been kidding when he said he wasn't much good at remembering school lessons, but with constant pounding into his head he was able to pass muster. Herb had never seriously thought about a teaching career, but after helping the guys survive their courses he could understand the satisfaction a teacher must feel when a student succeeds.

Delbert Finch was another story. It didn't take long for the entire barracks to see that Finch was the biggest popoff and screwball they had ever met. He had messmates shaking their heads constantly at the featherbrained things he said and did, had them laughing uproariously at the ribald jokes and imitations of CPO Adams—when Adams wasn't around, of course. Finch launched into a virtuoso parroting of Adams one night: "Men, this is the Navy! Not the Army, the Air Force, or the Marines, no, the Navy! You swabbies had better learn to clean this ship to my satisfaction or I am going to throw you overboard in the middle of the Pacific Ocean, where you can count on the sharks to find you and give you the once over before they begin to nibble at your little toes-ies. Yessir, you boys are in the Navy now, and if you think you can do what you want when you want, you got another thing comin'!!" Virgil, from Anadarko, Oklahoma, used a Southern phrase to describe Finch. "He's as goofy as a run-over dog." Few had heard that line before, but it sure fit. All Herb could think about Finch was, *There's one in every crowd, and the good Lord threw away the mold when He made that guy.* Not surprisingly, Finch earned the nickname Jughead. It sure fit him.

As they neared the end of their training, Herb grew a bit more anxious. Where was the next stop? He had originally assumed, since he was from the East coast, that the stormy Atlantic would be his next destination after training; but now he had gone West to serve in the Pacific. The most important thing to him was he wanted to serve in far off places, not near the shore in one of the small boats as part of the Donald Duck Navy that patrolled the U.S. coast. Most guys looked down on those who stayed stationed in the States. Herb didn't doubt their importance, but he had spent enough time near the East coast shoreline. He was ready to actually put to sea in a massive ship and experience ocean life to the full. One day he would look back ruefully at his naivete', but for now he was young, strong, and ready for anything—or so he thought.

It was nearly time to deploy, but Herb, Ollie, and Virgil were fired up. There was a show at Luce coming to the base, a "send-off" of sorts, headlined by Bob Hope and Nat King Cole. Herb especially was intrigued by Hope's comic timing and stage presence. He learned that Hope had a killer schedule, but was determined to bring some life and enjoyment to the guys who were sacrificing so much for their country. Casually swinging a golf club, Hope got several standing ovations, the first after only a few minutes on the stage. He was a master at the one-liner, Herb decided. He and his buddies also enjoyed the soulful, sometimes sad refrains from the already famous jazz singer and pianist Cole. They were amazed to discover he had done his first performance at four years of age when he played and sang *Yes, We Have No Bananas* for the crowd.

"Plenty of talent in those two show-stoppers," commented Ollie. It was obvious that all the boys on the base were enlivened and their morale boosted by the show. It was a good thing too, because Herb, Virgil, and Ollie had been assigned to the USS *Edwards*, a three hundred forty-eight-foot destroyer that had just been commissioned. With Herb's help, Ollie and Virgil had passed their "Battle Stations" comprehensive exam, and they were all sailors now, ready to become sea-lovin' old salts with fantastic stories to tell their grandchildren. *World War II, here we come!*

Chapter 8: Kit Bloodies a Lip

"There's only three places to go my friend—South Carolina, North Carolina, or the new one on the West Coast; Camp Pendleton in San Diego." Kit thought about what the Marine recruiter was saying. *"That's a long way south no matter which direction I head, but California is closer to Big Sky country than the southeast. So I say 'California, here I come!'"*

Arriving at Camp Pendleton early in the morning, Kit followed the line of men off the bus and began to experience the Marine way immediately. "Alright you boots, welcome to your new home away from home. Get in there and get your gear thrown into the barracks. Then Uncle Sam wants to feed you to let you know how well he's going to take care of you. I'm your DI, Corporal Danvers. DI stands for Drill Instructor, and we're going to get to know each other pretty well, because you are going to drill, and drill, and then drill some more." Danvers had the coldest, meanest set of eyes Kit had ever seen, besides those of the wolves and cougars he had hunted. It seemed the only reason Danvers didn't chew them up and spit them out right then was because he wanted to save them so the Japanese could do it later. *Well, Kit, thought, what did I expect, a parade in my honor when I got here?*

The food wasn't exactly anything to write home about, but there was plenty of it. The afternoon was a blur, with Kit given a medical checkup, inoculations, dog tags, ID cards, a service record book, a haircut, and then issued clothing, gear, and his very own rifle, an M1. At that point he was mostly a number instead of a name. They bundled up all his civilian clothing and personal belongings, left him only his wallet, and mailed the rest back to Montana. The men had to line up in alphabetical order for everything, and with the name Anderson he was always near the front of the line. Some guy near the middle was always razzing him and the others up front. "Hey, you fellows some kind of celebrities or something? What'd ya do, bribe the drill instructor already? How come we don't get first pick of the goodies?" One of the staff sergeants finally told the guy to knock it off, but Kit noticed him and reminded himself to stay away from the character anyway. What a jerk! Barely arrived and already there was some idiot making waves for no reason.

The alphabet wasn't involved when they lined up for chow, and Kit was glad. He'd had his fill of being up front. This time the loudmouth was several men ahead of him in line; but if he thought the wisenheimer would lay off, he was mistaken. Turning to Kit, he hooted, "Hey, big britches, guess who's in front now?" Kit wondered what kind of smart aleck went around just looking to get something started; wondered if maybe the guy's mouth had no off switch. He outweighed Kit by a good fifty pounds or more, but Kit had never taken bullying from anyone, and he decided that boot camp wasn't a good place to start. He figured he might as well get the confrontation over with sooner rather than later, like he'd done in elementary school and junior high. Everybody was sizing up everybody else, and a show of weakness would make the next seven weeks an intensely unhappy time for the man who allowed anyone to pick on him. He'd never liked the bottom of the totem pole anyway. Kit thought he'd deal with it later that night in the barracks.

As they began to settle in for the night, Kit noticed where loudmouth bunked, and was just going to go have a little talk with him when Corporal Danvers came in. Danvers was there to give them a reminder, "Gentlemen, Reveille is at 0400. For those of you still thinking like civilians, that's four o'clock in the *morning*. You probably don't need to be told to get some sleep while you can, but the Marines wanted to extend you every courtesy on your first day here. Now get your beauty rest. I promise you you'll need all the energy you can muster come morning."

Danvers left, but before he could hit the hay, Kit was ready for the inevitable head-to-head with his loudmouth comrade. It was in Kit's nature to deal with unpleasant things straight on rather than wait for a better time. The guy was yapping about something as usual when Anderson came up to him and told him he had something to say.

51

"Well, the little guy can talk after all! What's up, buttercup?"

Kit coolly responded, "Next time you talk to me like you been doing, I'm coming after you and I'm gonna shut your mouth."

"Oh really? Talking to you like what?" Bigmouth leaned in to make sure Kit understood how un-intimidated he was with his threat.

The next thing the loudmouth knew his lip was split open from a lightning quick punch. The guy hadn't even seen Kit move. Roaring like a bloodied bull, the big fellow swung back, but Kit sidestepped him and landed another jab to the face. Rage consumed the bigger man, and he tried again to knock Kit's head off, but the much smaller and quicker Kit had learned his boxing moves well, and the man had no chance. Kit cut him up again, then followed with a flurry to the stomach that knocked loudmouth to the floor, where he gasped for air.

Kit quietly turned and went back to his bunk and climbed in. The rest of his barracks-mates chuckled quietly to themselves and thought *there's a lot more to that little man than meets the eye.* Nobody bothered Anderson after that. If Kit was fighting to gain some respect, he had accomplished that—and how.

Danvers set them all straight the next day. "I heard you lads had a little excitement last night after I left. Hope you got some of the foolishness out of your system. Today we begin to learn that you are not each others' enemy. The Japanese are your enemy, and you need to learn to fight *them*. Learn the lessons well. Our objective is to drill them into you so much that you respond in combat without thinking too much about it. Too much thinking and hesitation at the wrong time gets a man killed."

Kit was actually excited about the drills. He had wanted to prove what he was made of, and this was the perfect place to do it. Over the next three weeks Corporal Danvers would take the boots on countless hours of hiking and physical training at all hours of the day and night. Sometimes they'd be awakened in the middle of the morning, even earlier than usual, for a night hike. There were grumblers aplenty, but Kit understood that in battle there was no telling what they might be asked to do, or when they would be asked to do it. He just wanted to demonstrate to everyone—especially himself—that he could handle whatever they could dish out. Fortunately he had been trained to hunt in the mountains, to suffer discomfort in silence, and to take pride in taking care of himself no matter what hardships came up. He was in much better shape, both physically and mentally, than most of his comrades.

Kit especially loved the rifle range, and he got plenty of practice there. He had handled guns from his infancy it seemed, and his M1 quickly became an extension of his body. He heard they had used '03 Springfield rifles for a long time in the Marine Corps, but finally came out with something more modern. Kit showed incredible marksmanship from the beginning, and earned the praise of Danvers. Danvers even asked him to show the other boots how to properly handle a gun.

What Kit couldn't get over was the bayonet. He tried to imagine using the ten-inch blade to gut a real live human being. And equally shocking was the thought that some Japanese soldier was going to try and stick *his* sixteen-inch blade into him! Maybe those guys had shot and dressed game there. Kit wondered if Japan had any elk or bear. There are some things in warfare that you just don't think about until you actually get in the battle. They were being trained to yell and bring that razor sharp blade up and into a man, but Kit wasn't sure any of them could do it when the actual time came. He sure wasn't looking forward to finding out the hard way.

The first full day's drills finally ended, and everyone was getting ready for evening chow. Walking toward the mess hall, the big loudmouth fellow sidled up alongside Kit. "Hey, Anderson, can I have a word with you?"

The sauce was gone from his voice, and Kit, a forgiving type by nature, replied, "Sure, how can I help you?"

"I just figured we got off on the wrong foot, and I know it's my fault. I was just nervous and showing off for the boys, you know."

"Well, I just knew I couldn't let anybody push me around, especially at the start. Hope I didn't break that beautiful face of yours."

"Naw...I been hit harder. This isn't the first time my mouth has gotten me in trouble. Say, where in the world did you learn to fight like that? I didn't come close to landing a punch." The bigger man seemed to genuinely admire the small boxer.

"I always been kinda small, so my dad figured I'd better learn to box. I fought bantamweight in early high school and lightweight my senior year. I had ballooned all the way up to a hundred thirty-two pounds."

"Is that so? Well, I can tell you were pretty good at it. Played football myself, though I wasn't much of a star. My name's Tasker, Tasker Meadows."

"Kit Anderson. Glad to meet you. Tasker is an unusual name, isn't it?"

"Yeah, my old man named me after Major General Tasker Bliss, Army Chief of Staff during the Great War. Dad served in the infantry, and he loves two things: his country and the history of warfare. Thought giving me a military name would make me happy to serve, I guess. Don't know if that's true, but I sure didn't want to be in the infantry like him. Too boring and you get shot at too much."

"You don't think the Marines will get shot at?"

"Well, sure, but at least there's more fame in being a Marine—it seems like the girls favor Marines over plain old Army grunts. At least that's why I signed up."

"So I guess we're o.k. now?" Kit didn't enjoy conflict, and hoped it was over.

"Sure," said Meadows. "I deserved the lickin' you gave me. I may talk too much, but one good thing about me is I know it. Besides, when a man needs someone to fight alongside, he might as well find one who can carry his own weight, even if the man is a lightweight."

Kit felt slighted again, and could feel the anger rising up in him, but Tasker noticed and diffused it quickly. "Hey, just kidding. I'll try to watch it about joshing you for your size. You carry more wallop per pound than anybody I know."

"Okay, Meadows, just be sure and remember this conversation, and watch it. As you may have noticed, I'm a bit sensitive about being the runt of the litter."

While they ate their grub, Tasker, who knew all about the Marines, told the rest of the boots at his table, "This training goes all the way back to nineteen eleven and Major

General William P. Biddle, Commandant of the Marine Corps. Biddle figured eight weeks of basic training would do, then they increased it to twelve weeks, but this war needed guys to throw into the line, so they shortened it to four weeks. Then the brilliant geniuses who run things learned half the gentlemen they had trained couldn't shoot their own foot off without more target practice, so they settled on seven weeks."

The subject of the bayonet came up, and somebody told them that the Japanese were trained not only to kill with their bayonets, but to torture as well. "Ever heard of the rape of Nanking?" a boot named Hack Wilson asked. "Them Japs killed tens of thousands of Chinese, after raping the women and torturing the men. Hung a bunch of them from trees and practiced bayonet drills on them. They were taught how to stab a man many times without killing him."

"How could people do that kind of thing?"

"Guess they hated the Chinese a bunch; and like all 'tough guys' from all of history, they wanted to make sure everybody was afraid of them."

"Well that would sure do it. Say, Hack is an interesting name." Kit had never met anyone named Hack before.

"The actual name is Henry James, but they've called me Hack since I was little 'cause it was easier to say when somebody needed me, usually because I was in trouble."

"Well Hack, call me Kit."

"I already know about you. That was quite a show you put on last night with Meadows."

Tasker heard his name, and piped up, "Hey, maybe Anderson can lick me because of his boxing skills, but nobody else better try anything like that. I can hold my own."

"Meadows, if you could just hold your own *tongue* it might do you some good. Then nobody else would have to make you bite it." Hack enjoyed seeing the big man squirm a bit.

Everyone laughed, even Tasker. "You got a point there Wilson, I have to admit." You had to say this about Tasker Meadows: he might let his mouth get him into trouble, but he also could see his own faults and admit them, and everyone appreciated that about him.

The next day Danvers picked up on the training schedule. "We used to give you knuckleheads twelve weeks to learn how to be soldiers, which wasn't really enough time. Now you've got to learn it in seven weeks. So you need to learn as fast and thoroughly as you can what used to take almost twice as long to learn, because your life will depend on performing what you've learned—and the life of the guy next to you will depend on you doing it too."

Kit noticed a guy that first week who was as nervous as could be. He'd seen the fellow actually shed a tear or two;

seemed scared to death. Kit made it a point to introduce himself.

"Hey, I'm Kit Anderson from near Missoula, Montana. Who are you?"

"Walter Horn from near Madison, Wisconsin."

"Least we're both from the north. Why'd you choose the Marines, Walter?"

"My dad thought it'd be the best place to turn me into a man."

"Well, it's a tough place for sure. They're trying to turn us undisciplined kids into fighting men that will do our country proud. Part of the way they do that is to take away our individuality and make us obey promptly when given an order. Did you hear about the barracks next to ours? Their DI, Sergeant Ryker, took a box of chocolate chip cookies some mom had sent her boy, and made the boys stand at attention while he ate the entire box one at a time. Seems cruel, but they have their reasons for the way they do everything I suppose."

"Hope I have what it takes to make Dad proud. We've only been here a week but it sure seems lonesome and I miss the folks." Walter bowed his head and had a faraway look in his eyes.

Kit said, "You'll do fine, Walter. These things are new for all of us, but I'm confident we'll all come through. If you ever want to talk, look me up."

Kit enjoyed the last two weeks of training probably more than any other time, because the recruits had extended time on the rifle range, plus they got to practice with machine guns and had opportunity to drive half-tracks, trucks with trailers, and jeeps through obstacle courses. Kit realized they might be asked to do almost anything at any time, and the brass wanted them to have some experience before they were asked to do it. There was a lot more training on hand-to-hand combat as well. Using a knife in combat was mercilessly drilled into their heads, and they had many sessions on survival skills. Danvers told them, "You never know when you're going to have to survive in the jungle without reinforcements, and with the Japanese right next door. We can't prepare you for everything, but we're doing our best to think of most things and pray you'll figure out what to do when the time comes."

As they neared the end of their time at Pendleton, they began to focus on new drills: obstacle courses, improvising rope bridges, and seemingly endless practice sessions for debarking from ships via cargo nets onto Higgins Boats and then hitting the beach. Danvers, as always, had words of advice for them. "The Germans and the Japanese have grown up with war; thinking about it, training for it, experiencing it. You haven't had that luxury. It's all new to you…in a sense new to most of us in the States. You're going to fight the Nips, and they are from a warrior society. They don't think you *can* fight, that you are too soft. I've done my best to make you tougher, to get you ready to prove them wrong."

Danvers last words to them struck Kit hard. "You are going to be afraid in combat. A lot of you are probably afraid you'll be so afraid that you won't be able to do your job. I've tried to prepare you to do your job regardless of how afraid you are. And just keep this in mind. You aren't alone in being afraid. Everybody's afraid. The ones who aren't afraid are the ones who get killed first. I hate to tell you all this, but I'm sure you know it already. Some of you are going to die in this war. When you joined up nobody promised you that you would ever get to come home again. But there's no use crying about it. It also is a good idea to make no friends. War is hard enough as it is, and when you lose a friend it's even worse. I wish you all the best of luck, and maybe you'll live long enough for me to see you again someday."

Initially Kit had disliked Danvers' gruff ways, those cold, ruthless wolf eyes that seemed to see only victims to be torn to pieces. He had thought maybe the only reason Danvers hadn't ripped them limb from limb was so he could save them for the Japs to take care of it for him. But as time went on he began to see more and more method behind the madness of the training, and he respected Danvers for it. He intuitively realized that during the heat of battle the hardness of their bodies and their ability to obey instantly could mean the difference between coming back home alive or being buried on a faraway Pacific island. He realized that Danvers did really care about the men, and was burdened by the fact that not all of them would come home alive and well. *I owe it to him that I am now a Marine,* Kit thought. *He's taught me that nothing matters so little as my own personal likes and dislikes. Now, it's all about the team and the team's objectives.*

George Dickens, a slender six-foot beanpole from Colorado, one of Kit's favorites since they were both mountain boys, smiled at Wilson and Anderson and said, "Boys, our play days are over. Now we can start earning our money."

"Where do we go from here?" asked Bennie Friedman, the big bear of a man from New Jersey.

Kit answered, "Didn't you pay attention to the memo they sent out? We're going to New Zealand for final preparation to storm some beach in the middle of the Pacific Ocean."

"New Zealand?! I don't even know where that is."

"Well, you'd better get a map and find it, 'cause that's where we're headed. It's a big island near Australia. That will be our jumping off place…jumping off to who knows where."

Chapter 9: First Run

Tank had been in the military long enough now to expect changes, but he really didn't understand what the guys in charge were thinking, and he didn't mind telling Dixon all about it. "Look, we trained on B-17's. They're easier to get off the ground, easier to fly, and easier to land; plus they don't break up or sink if you gotta ditch into the Pacific."

"Yeah", responded Dixon, "but the B-24 is a man's plane; it's not for sissies. You gotta have some muscle to fly this baby. They don't call it the 'Flying Box Car' for nothin'. You were made to fly this thing, Tank."

"I heard somebody call it the 'Flyin' Brick', which just about sums up how easy it is to get off the ground and keep in the air."

"Well then Tank, looks like you get to fly a tank now."

"It fits you Tank", added Tom Lancaster, "cause it takes Superman to fly the thing. I've known some guys that were so spent after a long mission that they had to be helped out of the seat by their crew."

Tank responded, "Man, I feel like I've gotta feather the thing constantly to keep it in trim. It sure takes its own sweet time responding to the controls. Almost seems like *it* wants to be in control. Have the engineers who designed this thing ever taken one up?"

Dixon finished with the comment, "It may be a son-of-a-gun to fly, but it can take a heavier bomb load farther and faster than any plane we have, and we need it to carry the fight to the Japs."

Eventually Tank got the hang of it, and finally he embraced the challenge of handling the big machine. Something about the lumbering old thing made him feel sort of reassured and secure, except for the thought that when even a single engine went out, you were in big trouble, and they didn't mean some time later, but right now. Oh, and the troubling problem that sometimes its new wings tended to fold up and break off when hit by a shell. Other than that, everything was fine.

"Man, the thing weighs thirty-two thousand pounds without anything in it. Fully loaded, it weighs sixty thousand pounds. And you've got to get it into the air. I'm just glad I'm not the pilot." Lancaster was training to be a gunner, and he was in awe of the B-24's specifications.

But Dixon added, "The nice thing is it will fly three hundred miles an hour, and can go up to thirty-two thousand feet. Plus it's loaded with ten fifty-caliber machine guns. At least we can fight back if they come for us!" Dixon hadn't passed his pilot training, but had become a first-class navigator, and Tank was sure excited to have his old friend around.

Tank considered, "We could take four one-ton bombs, eight thousand-pound bombs, twelve five-hundred-pound bombs, or twenty hundred-pound bombs. Or a partridge in a pear tree, whichever we choose." So Tank learned to pilot "The Flying Coffin." He just hoped he'd never have to be buried in the thing.

The American Army Air Force had a policy. Every rookie pilot had to fly his first five combat missions as a co-pilot with a veteran pilot and experienced crew. Tank didn't complain. Nervous enough as he was, he didn't relish the idea of having all those other lives dependent on him in battle just quite yet. Tank was lucky too. On his first assignment he flew with the best pilot on the base, Captain Mark (Slim) Connors, all of twenty-six-years-old at the time, just three years older than Tank, but already a veteran of thirty-six missions over Japanese targets. Connors was smart, cool-headed, and pleasant, the kind of man who didn't mind being asked questions by a nervous rookie; a man who liked to teach.

The day of the mission Tank was awakened by the operations sergeant at four a.m. Senses tingling, he got dressed and headed to the mess hall for powdered eggs and coffee, then climbed into the back of a truck for the ride to the briefing. At the door an MP looked at his identification, checked his name on the roster, and let him in. There were crewmen everywhere, close to one hundred of them. When roll call finished and all were accounted for, Colonel Bridges, the group commander, a grizzled old man in his forties, strode in and up to the platform with a determined look in his eyes.

"Men, the Japanese are causing havoc everywhere in the Pacific theater, including Burma. They've attacked Rangoon relentlessly, now occupy a good portion of it, and are working on a railway to link their bases to it once they've completely captured it. We must not allow them to finish this railway. We are going to deliver them a few tons of explosives as a June Christmas present and slow them up a bit. You've heard perhaps that we will be teaming up with the RAF on these missions, with a group that have dubbed themselves "Burma Bombers." A few of the boys in this outfit are Canadians, so all you Northern fellows will be working with your neighbors. Intel says British, Canadian, and Australian POWs constitute a lot of the slave labor for the enemy construction projects. Let's pay the Japs back for using our friends like coolies."

Tank suited up and was introduced to the crew. Tom Brewer was the tail gunner, from Lubbock, of all places. Tank and he were both pretty excited to see another Texan in the outfit. Jack Gregory was the bombardier, from Gallup, New Mexico. Tank couldn't believe it; another guy from the Southwest. But Eddie Conrad, the radio operator, was from Ohio; Jug Whitehead, the navigator, hailed from White

Plains, New York; the belly gunner was actually an ex-Canadian named Charles Miller; the engineer and other gunner were from Oregon. Despite growing up in very different parts of the country, and despite major differences in personality and philosophy, this crew had been on the last ten runs together, and they were a tight-knit group. It was critical that it be that way. Seemingly little things like accents, phrases, the comics or books they liked, the way they brushed their teeth; little things can get magnified out of all proportion when you cram a bunch of guys together for extended periods of time, training together, and especially under the added stress of war. But because everyone's life and health depended on everyone else doing their job, as long as the men were competent, they were accepted and the guys learned to trust each other. They would build bonds stronger than any civilians would ever know. These guys shared that bond, and Tank was the stranger in their midst. But they accepted him quickly, and he felt comfortable with them.

Once they were seated in the pilot and co-pilot seats Slim Connors explained: "One lesson you gotta learn early, and that is you take care of your buddies and they take care of you. I've trained, lived, bunked, eaten, worked, played, and been to war with these guys; we share our lives until death or until the war ends."

Tank wondered out loud, "What if one of the guys is a jerk or doesn't do his job right?"

"We ask the brass to dump them, and fast," replied Slim. "We had a waist-gunner who was an alcoholic, and we couldn't trust him. We went to the higher ups as a crew and asked for the guy to be sent packing, and they did it. They know the damage something like that can cause on a mission, and how it can ruin the team's morale, or even cost all of us our lives. We lose enough planes and crews as it is."

Each B-24 revved its engines and got in line for takeoff. Tank was excited, nervous, and wide-eyed. He now was a proficient pilot, but this was his first taste of actual combat, and he was understandably emotional. No training can adequately prepare a man for warfare, the supreme test, even though the trainers had done their best to do so. The first run was the first run, and nothing else would ever be quite like this day.

The crew was bundled up, even in this tropical climate during the summer, because their plane would fly at altitudes where it was bitterly cold, with open windows in the waist, making the waist gunners and tail gunner miserable, and their equipment and clothing covered with a layer of frost. In addition, since the B-24 wasn't pressurized, everyone had to wear their ill-fitting rubber oxygen masks above about ten thousand feet. All the men had electrically heated flight suits they could plug into rheostats, but when the system shorted out, which it often did, the suits were useless, so the added layers of bulky clothing made the plane seem even more claustrophobic than it already was. Tank of course was delighted that he got to sit up front away from all the closeness. Just the thought of being squeezed together with the others gave him the cold sweats, even before they reached high altitude.

His cold sweats were just starting, as it turned out. Flying above the designated target, the Japanese anti-aircraft began to speak. It was Tank's first exposure to flak, and it wasn't a pleasant experience. He would see large puffs of black smoke, hear the explosions, feel the concussion as the plane flew through, and hear the pieces of shrapnel ping against the aluminum skin of the plane. Connors said he'd get used to it, there was nothing that could be done about it anyway, but Tank sure wished somebody would think of something they could do to protect themselves a bit more. Flak was essentially an eighty-eight-millimeter shell exploding, sending red-hot pieces of metal in all directions—red-hot metal that penetrated the skin of their plane with ease. Connors said the mechanics had bolted an extra thick piece of iron to the bottom of their seats, so at least they had a bit more security for their posteriors, but to show how lucky you sometimes had to be to survive flak bursts, Slim bent over to check out a gauge that didn't seem to be working right when a piece of spent flak went right through the windshield and banged against the parachute buckle at his back. Had his head been where it was previously, he would have lost an eye or been killed.

"Get used to it, huh!?" Tank was visibly shaken.

Slim smiled, "Well, it's why there is no shortage of prayer before we come up, and while we're flying. Flyboys are closer to God than anybody else in war, probably in every way."

Tank could certainly verify that he had been praying a lot lately, and repeating Psalm twenty-three: *Yea, though I walk through the valley of the shadow of death, I will fear no evil; for Thou art with me; Thy rod and Thy staff, they comfort me...* He realized it really was a comfort to remind himself of God's care, even here on another continent far from home, over twenty thousand feet above the earth.

Connors had turned things over to the navigator and bombardier, and the bombs were released without incident. Thankfully the Japanese air force had been depleted to a large degree, and most of their available fighters were helping guard Rangoon, so no Zeroes showed up to molest them as they turned for home. It seemed their run had been successful, but recon planes would take pictures to verify how much of the railway had been damaged by their sortie.

Something else happened on the way home that seared itself into Tank's memory. Flying in formation was critical, and the hardest thing about flying in the war. There were dozens of planes, sometimes several layers of them, and if everyone didn't hold their place, disaster could occur. After the bombs were dropped planes could peel off and get away from the flak to head for home, but today one of the bombers inexplicably changed altitude as it wheeled away, and it flew right in front of another bomber. There was a horrifying crash, and bits of planes and bodies began falling through the Asian sky. Two planes, two crews—gone, just like that; eighteen men dead because of pilot error. Tank looked at Slim, who had closed his eyes for a moment, then slowly shook his head from side to side. It shook Tank deeply, and the responsibility of taking care of the men who would make up his crew, if not already hammered deep into his psyche, was pounded there with renewed vigor. In training there was so much to think about, so much to remember; but now Tank realized that a large part of war was not the remembering, but the forgetting you could never do. That night as he shut his eyes to pray and sleep, he could still see those men falling, falling through the sky to their deaths. *How he prayed he would never be the unwitting cause of a buddy's death. Dear Lord, please help me always do my best.*

Chapter 10: The Worst Kind of War

Herb struggled with his emotions. He had been taught by tolerant parents to be tolerant of others, empathetic of their situations. Raised in the Presbyterian Church, he was instructed from his earliest days to love others as Christ loved, and he had tried to follow that creed throughout his young life. As far as he could tell his father and mother didn't have a prejudiced bone in their bodies, and he hoped that was true of him as well. Herb had reasoned that though other people might not believe as he did, he could get along with anyone if he could understand them and try to show them that he understood.

But now he was bombarded by attitudes toward the Japanese he found disconcerting. His fellow sailors were full of pent-up animosity toward the whole Japanese race, and they made their sentiments known loudly, and often.

"Bunch of miserable barbarians, that's all they are."

"Snarling rats needing extermination, is what I say."

"Slanty-eyed demons from hell."

"I heard Admiral Halsey has a new slogan: 'Kill Japs, kill Japs, kill more Japs.' As for me, I aim to do my part!"

For Herb's part, it was all unnerving and troubling. Naturally kind-hearted and generous, it was impossible to square his convictions with the vitriol hurled at the as yet unseen enemy. He wanted to serve his country, was compelled to help his country, but to think of others as less than human couldn't be a good thing, he reasoned.

The differences between the Japanese culture and American culture were starkly highlighted in U.S. Navy training sessions. Most Americans were Christians, at least nominally so, who had been taught that they were sinful mortals who needed a savior. But the Japanese had been raised to believe that god blood flowed through their veins, that they had a direct connection to the heavens, that it was their manifest destiny to conquer not only their islands, but China, India, Siberia and the entire Pacific, to meld these lands under Japanese rule as the "eight corners of the world under one roof", the doctrine of *Hakko Ichiu.* Americans talked of living in a land blessed by God. Japanese believed they lived in a land *of* the gods. Nineteenth century Americans believed they were destined by God to conquer the West and inhabit a continent. The Japanese believed they were divinely destined to rule their part of the world.

For most of Japanese history they had lived a very isolated existence on an island archipelago, so these beliefs had been strengthened by many generations who had experienced no pushback from the world around them. To affirm the belief that they were destined to conquer and rule, all they had to do was open their eyes in the morning. Didn't the sun rise first on their land, and then on to the rest of creation? Japan's very name for itself was Nippon, from *ni*,

74

for sun, and *pon*, meaning origin. They were the land of the rising sun. So they were special. And sadly, all others were *gaizin*, the name for foreigner, which in their language literally meant *"the outside people."* Since the beginning of time men had warred with one another, in large part by stereotyping and demonizing the "other." In this war the Japanese and Americans would take it to the extreme. To many Japanese their enemies weren't just outside Japan, they were outside humankind; they were non-human.

And it didn't help matters that the U.S. military felt it their duty to gin up resentment and ire among their forces for the fight against them. True, Japan had treacherously attacked Pearl Harbor even while their ambassadors were speaking peace with Washington, and true they had killed thousands of Americans when the countries were not officially at war. But the trainings painted every Japanese as a buck-toothed Neanderthal, a brute who, if not non-human, was at least portrayed as sub-human. It was enough to stir an already hot fire into a maelstrom of anger and hatred. There was hardly a sailor aboard, including the officers, who didn't want revenge against the *dirty Japs.*

Herb understood that, if war was hell, this was going to be the worst kind of hell, with unrestrained hellish behavior on both sides. Once he had realized his assignment was the Pacific theater, Herb had studied some Japanese history, and he realized right away differences between Japanese and

American culture that were going to make mutual understanding almost impossible. As their history unfolded, the Japanese had given up individual rights for stability. There were thousands of rules of etiquette, actual laws listing varieties of dress appropriate for everyone from the lowest serf to the emperor. Unbelievably, the size, shape, and color of the very stitches in the clothing were specified. What kind of houses each class could build, what they could buy to eat, who they bowed to and when, where they could travel—they had laws that governed the very tiniest details of their lives. It was the most regimented society in the world.

Americans on the other hand were the freest people on earth, and chafed at even the smallest restrictions on that freedom. They wore what they wanted, ate anything they could afford, went wherever they wished whenever they wished. The thought of bowing to a government official in any circumstance was laughable. *I'm just as good as they are! I can say what I want, and nobody can tell me how to live my life! Says so in the Bill of Rights!*

The Japanese had no bill of rights. They were the emperor's subjects, the *shinmin*, the *obedient ones.* The entire Japanese military structure was based on climbing the ladder so you could beat into subjection the ones beneath you. Herb found in his study that it wasn't uncommon for Japanese officers to beat the daylights out of subordinates for routine infractions, or just because they had the power to do so. There was no idea of "fairness" within the Japanese military. Americans wouldn't have stood very long for physical abuse from an officer. It would have been a very quick rebellion indeed had any of the officers tried hitting men with a baseball bat, as the Japanese officers reportedly did. In fact, Japanese officers referred to draftees as *issen gorin*, the cost of a postcard telling the family that their son had died for the emperor. To Japanese officers men were cannon fodder to use however they wished in battle and then discarded as soon as they were used up.

American soldiers and sailors believed they served in a sort of meritocracy, where they could rise by stint of hard work and ability; but the Japanese grunts served in more of a slave society than anything else. Those at the bottom of this brutal totem pole were non-persons, and those above them treated them as such. The life of the individual was worth little. The emperor, and the code for which he stood, was everything. As a result Japanese soldiers and sailors were supposed to gladly die for the cause; and many of Herb's comrades were glad to make that happen if they could, but far fewer of the American sailors thought it so glorious to die for America's cause. Their dreams of going home again, of having a life again after the military, those were the dreams that kept some of them going as they sailed into the unknown.

As Herb studied he discovered, to no great astonishment, that the children were taught early in life the expected code of their respective societies. For many years Japanese public schools had taught extreme patriotism and martial contemplation. *"Military spirit education"* was emphasized, and all good and faithful subjects were encouraged to give up their own individuality for the good of the state. All facets of the school curriculum were filled with emperor worship and militarism. The *first grade* reader had pictures of soldiers with the words *Advance! Advance! Soldiers move forward!* Not surprisingly, a popular song among Japanese children said:

There is a Law of Nations it is true

But when the moment comes, remember

The Strong eat up the Weak

Herb compared the attitudes of Japanese children with what he had been taught in church when he was a child:

Jesus loves the little children

All the children of the world

Red and yellow, black and white

They are precious in His sight

Jesus loves the little children of the world

Herb now saw why Americans spent so much money on Christian missions, and why the Japanese spent so much money on armament and war. Japan, with so small a slice of the world's landmass, always was looking for more room to expand. They were always in need of more raw materials, and they had long felt threatened by the Russians and the Chinese, so Chinese resources beckoned to help sate their colonial hungers.

The Japanese had always hated the Chinese, it seemed. They had a long laundry list of perceived Chinese grievances, and they were taught by their officers to treat the Chinese as *kichiku*—devils. Herb even read that the army infantry textbooks of nineteen thirty-three included this entry about prisoners: *"If you kill them, there will be no repercussions."* Talk about a green light for genocide!

No wonder they had killed hundreds of thousands of Chinese in nineteen thirty-seven and thirty-eight in the Rape of Nanking. Herb read one account of a second lieutenant who came into that Chinese conflict reticent to slaughter the enemy, but was taught the proper way to bayonet the enemy, cut off the head of the prisoner-of-war, and commit unspeakable atrocities against Chinese women and children. The pressure to succumb to those rapacious instincts was great. Few Japanese soldiers could restrain themselves from abusing those in their power, because they had suffered abuse from those above them in authority. The Rape was only a few years ago, and Herb realized that the same perverted warrior spirit on full display in China inhabited the sailors he would meet in battle. It made him glad to be on a ship where his closest contact with a Japanese soldier or sailor would likely be while shooting at him from several miles away. It gave him the shivers to think of being face-to-face with them and at their mercy.

Chapter 11: Battle

"New Guinea. Why are we here Kit?"

"Don't know, Johnny, the Aussies need our help I guess."

"Yeah," added Meadows, "they've been here for more than a year fighting tooth and nail, trying to battle their way over the Owen Stanley Mountains. Least we can do is help 'em along a bit."

"Somebody told me he heard the colonel say holding New Guinea was central to the Japanese strategy for the war. That means two things: one is they've poured lots of troops, ships, and warplanes into the effort; the other is that we've got to go and knock them all out." George said this with a grim but determined look on his face.

Kit took a long look at the beach. Less than a hundred yards behind it was thick jungle, hiding the enemy. Even though it was November the air was humid and warm, and sweat was already rolling down Kit's body. *This ain't no Montana winter, and we ain't going to need our overcoats.* The ships' big guns had been pounding the enemy positions for a couple of hours now, the concussions rocking the craft and adding to the seasickness most of them already experienced. Kit thought for a mountain man they couldn't have picked a worse way for him to prepare for the fight of his life, putting him on this huge rocking horse swaying back and forth. A lot of the guys could handle the rocking, or the smells, or the confined spaces, but they couldn't handle them all at once. And the one truism about seasickness was that almost nobody could handle watching others get seasick without it affecting them too.

As Kit watched the bombardment, he wondered how any human being could survive it, and hoped like all his buddies that there would be little resistance when they hit the beach. The command was given to pack up and get ready to fill the Higgins' boats. Kit had hated all the practice going down those cargo nets back at Pendleton, but now he was glad he'd had lots of experience at it. *Why can't the ship just stay still for a bit so he wouldn't get squashed up against the side of it while trying to go down that netting?* Well, he wanted to be a Marine, and this is what Marines do, and now is the time we've all prepared to do it. As he descended the nets, loaded down with eighty pounds of equipment, he realized watching the men below him that he would have to time his jump off the bottom of the nets to coincide with the maximum rise of the boat on the swell; otherwise he would fall way too far and hurt himself or others. He sucked in his breath, counted to three, and let go. Fortunately his timing was good, even though he landed hard and was only prevented from being bowled over by several pairs of hands helping him to steady himself. The guy above him wasn't so lucky. He mistimed his jump and fell about twelve feet, landing on several other

Marines, and being roundly cursed in the process. He twisted his ankle as he hit, and had a hard time standing. *How in the world will he storm a beach like that? It's going to be hard enough as it is.*

Kit watched as another Marine wasn't even that lucky. He slipped and fell, missing the boat entirely, and sank to be seen no more. With all that equipment weighing him down he didn't stand a chance. It made Kit sick to his stomach. Here the man had dreamed of helping his country, had sacrificed to train, had disciplined himself for the invasion, and now he was gone without using his skills at all. *What a waste.* The landing craft shoved off, and soon terrifying sounds were all around him. The boom of enemy artillery pieces and explosions were seemingly everywhere; the sound of machine guns rattling and the detonation of mortar shells played a shrill cacophony on Kit's senses; the shrieking sound of incoming ordnance was unnerving. *Apparently there were plenty of enemy left on the island after the intensive shelling.* There was no way to assess it all, no ability to think much about anything except home and family and wondering if he'd ever get back there again. Not much had ever made Kit afraid, but he couldn't fool himself. He was scared stiff, and silently prayed.

Because of his height he could barely see out of the boat, and didn't want to stick his head up anyway; he could hear the pinging of bullets and shrapnel striking the sides of the

Higgins, and he didn't want one of those bullets between his eyes. Then a shell scored a direct hit on the boat next to his, and the concussion almost rocked him off his feet. The boat flew into the air, and he saw part of its graceful arc. It was there one moment, and the next it was gone, and with it the jeep and twelve-man squad in it. He didn't know any of those men personally, but he had seen them loading up, and knew that they were just like him. He kept thinking of one of his father's favorite phrases, "There but for the grace of God go I." *At least they hadn't suffered,* he thought, and though it was small comfort, except for the agitation and dread they had all experienced before this day of battle even began, *they hadn't even known what hit them.* That to him was the worst part of it all; *knowing* you could die, or worse, *anticipating* you could be horribly wounded, and screaming for a medic while you lay dying in agony. *In a way, those men who were vaporized were lucky, beyond the horror now; and it only took an instant.*

He remembered something else, something they had taught him at training; *make no real friends, because when you lose them it's all the harder; and war is hard enough as it is.* That was impossible of course. Meadows and he had started out on the wrong foot, but now he enjoyed Tasker's company as much as anybody he'd ever known. Hack Wilson, Bennie Friedman, George Dickens, Johnny Daniels; he just gravitated towards these guys. He liked them all, and

84

now they had been boots together, had traveled together, had trained for this assault together. They had laughed and even cried a bit together. Kit knew about their parents, their girlfriends, their likes and dislikes. *Don't make friends?* He hated to admit it, but these guys were now some of the best friends he'd ever had, despite only knowing them for a few months. He couldn't stand the thought of losing any of them.

"Prepare to debark," came the voice of the lieutenant driving their Higgins boat. *This is it,* Kit thought. *Please, dear Lord, help me make it across that beach.* The ramp came down and the confusion was immediate. One soldier in front of Kit was hit by ordnance and with a scream fell into the surf. Other Marines were yelling at the top of their lungs, hoping the emotional energy might somehow deflect bullets headed their way. A Marine named Thomas, who Kit had just talked to for a few minutes on board ship, was cut down and struggled to get back up as the waters covered him. Kit knew that with his heavy equipment strapped on to him, if the bullets hadn't killed him the water would. With all the weight he had to carry Kit struggled to move, and it seemed they were all going in slow motion, the outrushing tide pulling them back, the men behind them screaming for them to move forward; a few screaming for a medic's help. He saw several bodies floating in the surf, some of them without heads or arms or legs. *At least they were beyond pain now.*

Shaking with fear and excitement, memories of the horrors he had just witnessed fresh in his mind, Kit tried to block it all out so he could concentrate on the next phase of the operation. The men who had died or were wounded on the beach didn't seem real anymore in a way, just ghosts of a past life, even though they had been comrades and companions only moments ago. Kit only knew he was alive, unhurt, and that he didn't know how long either of those things were going to last. All he could do was try to remember his training and trust the good Lord to help him do his duty. Corporal Danvers' words came back to him from Camp Pendleton, "Too much thinking and hesitation at the wrong time gets a man killed." He certainly didn't want to die, but he knew that was an all-too-real possibility. Worse was the thought that any mistake he made could lead to the death of one of his buddies.

He was also fully aware that he had still not fired his rifle at a living human being in anger, or used his bayonet, and he wondered what that would be like. It wouldn't be long before he was going to find out.

Wilson and Daniels found Kit and joined him at the edge of the jungle under the trees. Kit wondered if his eyes were as wide as theirs. He didn't know if they qualified as veterans just yet, but after the last few minutes they were surely rookies no longer. They weren't sure about this island invasion strategy given them by the brass; it just seemed a good way for generals to commit their men to slaughter, like it had always been in war from the beginning; but since they were now here and alive, they knew they needed to get moving.

"Now what do we do?" asked Daniels. "What's the next step?"

Hack Wilson responded, "Well, knocking out some machine gun nests wouldn't be a bad idea."

"Right," said Kit. "I don't want it to be like WWI. They basically waited in trenches for the other guys to come find them, or for a mortar shell to land on their head. I'd like to do something to the enemy before he does it to me. You see any of the other guys?"

"I saw Lieutenant Sheets and a couple of the guys scurry for cover over on our right flank a few minutes ago. Maybe we should try and find them."

Sounded good to Kit, so they eased from behind the tree, no shots fired at them, and they began to skirt the jungle's edge and look for Sheets and the others. They didn't have to go far to find them. Hack nearly got himself shot by Tasker Meadows, who was next to Sheets and was as jumpy as a young deer surrounded by wolves.

"Put that gun down, Meadows, you're pointing it the wrong way!"

"Sorry, Wilson. I guess I'm a little nervous."

Hack added, "Well, join the rest of us."

Kit and Daniels came up, and Kit was glad to see Bennie Friedman and George Dickens there as well as Meadows and the lieutenant. At least some of his closest buddies had made it to this point, alive and well. And look who else made it— Walter from Wisconsin! Kit couldn't help but smile a bit. He figured if anyone would get killed quickly it would be Walter, but here he was, shaking, miserable beyond words, but alive.

The lieutenant gathered them together and reminded them, "Look, the Nips have dug-in positions, they've built pillboxes for protection, and they know we're coming. But we have to clean out those nests or we're just going to keep getting mowed down. Fix bayonets and follow me."

Kit was scared to death. It was the moment he had dreaded, all the way back at boot camp. His hands shook as he positioned his bayonet on the end of his rifle. Sweat was pouring down his face as he thought about using that long knife to kill a man. But they were on the move now, and he tried to think of nothing except obeying orders and doing his duty.

The squad didn't make a lot of sound as they crept through the jungle, everyone's nerves on high alert. With all the noise of the big guns still firing, no enemy could have heard them anyway. Kit saw Lieutenant Sheets give the hand down signal to alert them that he had spotted something. They were near the edge of a cleared area, and they noticed that a few bodies were laying there, probably killed not too long ago. Sheets made them understand that they were to rush the position all at once, and that they were to yell like madmen as they did so.

Lord, help me to do my duty! There was a sudden flash of steel as Sheets screamed at the top of his lungs and burst into the clearing. For a couple of moments as the men poured out and charged the guns there was silence, then the wild brrrpp-brrop of the machine gun firing at them. Two of the marines threw hand grenades into the pillbox, and for a blessed few seconds the guns ceased; only to begin again as new Japs manned the weapons. Men fell around Kit. Daniels spun around and hit the ground, bullets in his shoulder and left side. Friedman got hit multiple times and was blown over backwards as if decked by a strong uppercut. But the rest of them got through somehow, bayonets raised high.

There were five enemy soldiers still alive in the pillbox, and Sheets dove right into the middle of them. Bayonets were flashing in the light, and Kit found himself face-to-face with a small soldier about his size. The soldier's eyes were wide with terror as Kit raised the blade and drove it into his chest. Thankfully the man died quickly; it had been an accurate strike.

And in a few moments it was over. The five warriors from Nippon lay dead on the jungle floor. Kit looked at his friends and noticed a crazed look in some of their eyes. It was the first time they'd spilled a man's blood too. Sheets called Kit to come help him, and they went back to check on Daniels and Friedman. There was no hope for Bennie—he was dead before he hit the ground, probably never knew what hit him. But Johnny was alive, and Kit could see he was as mad as a wet hen. "Broke my shoulder, and a rib, and hurts like crazy." But he was alive, and apparently no vitals had been punctured. Sheets called up Wilson to help Kit get Daniels back toward the edge of the jungle where he might find a medic. Kit and his fellow Marines had tasted their first battle. They had killed other men. *They were combat veterans now.*

Chapter 12: Aftermath

Lieutenant Sheets told the men to dig in for the night. They had pushed the Imperial Japanese Army back, but certainly there would be much more fighting before they had them on the run. Everyone was nervous about counterattacks, especially at night in the jungle, where even in the daylight a man couldn't see much.

Kit and Tasker dug a big foxhole, and decided to alternate rounds of sleep and watch. Kit was first to try his hand at watching, to try to prevent any surprises, but as the gloom deepened he realized it was almost impossible to see anything in this dense jungle. The moon wasn't full, but had it been so there wasn't enough light to tell what in the world was going on out there. The foliage was just too thick. It made him extremely nervous. And the jungle night noises didn't help his raw nerves either. Used to hunting in the woods, sometimes at night, he still was unbalanced by the unearthly sounds that were nothing like anything he had heard in the Montana and Idaho mountains. After a couple of uneventful but anxious hours he woke Meadows and told him it was his turn to keep an eye out.

Bennie was dead. Kit couldn't help but remember that first day of battle, how they'd all survived the beach to storm the machine gun nest. Johnny had been wounded and removed to the ship hospital, but Bennie hadn't finished the charge, and now he was gone. Hack, who had been Friedman's best friend, had squatted down, taken Friedman's hand, and sat there a full five minutes, looking intently in Bennie's face. He never uttered a sound the whole time he was there. Tasker came and stood by the body, bent over, and spoke in a hoarse whisper as though Bennie could hear him. "So sorry, guy." He gently straightened the shirt collar of their fallen comrade, and walked away to be alone with his thoughts. They wrapped Friedman's body in the flag, and it was time to bury him. Sheets led out in reciting the Lord's Prayer, and the earth received its own.

Don't make friends. How could you keep from making friends? Abraham Lincoln once said that the better part of a man's life consists in his friendships. Kit understood that having friends opened you up to more pain, but it also kept you alive. Without friends you had to face all the horrors alone, and you couldn't face them that way—not and have anything left of yourself anyway.

The artillery shells had stopped booming, and darkness was complete in the jungle. They had dug in and set up a perimeter. Lieutenant Sheets warned them that the Japs did not rest at night, but skirmished to find unwary Marines they could kill. The Americans were so exhausted they had to sleep, but this news set them on edge again, and there were whispered conversations among those who shared a foxhole.

As Meadows woke to start his watch he wanted to know what Kit was thinking.

"What do I think? Where do I start? How do you even put words to what we've been through, words to describe what I fear we might go through tomorrow?"

Tasker, usually at no loss for words, muttered, "Yeah, what we think of war and what it really is are kind of two different things. I can't figure out why my Dad seemed to love it so much."

"Seeing men die is hard", Kit responded, "even when it's the enemy. At least we know now that we can overcome our fears and fight...and kill when we need to."

Tasker answered, "I had all these notions of what it would be like to kill a man, but none of them were what I felt when the time finally came. I guess it's either them or us, and I don't want to bury any more of my friends."

Kit thought about that long and hard, and he had to agree with Meadows. *It's either them or us. Better their folks get a sad letter than my folks,* he reasoned.

It seemed to take forever, but finally Kit fell into a fitful sleep. The bayonet was still attached to his M1, and he held it pointed up so that it would be ready if there was some crazy *banzai* charge in the middle of the night. Apparently Meadows was dozing too when all of a sudden Kit was aroused by a violent thrashing motion from his gun and a hysterical scream that pierced the silent darkness. What in the world is happening?! And then it dawned on him as a writhing body crashed into the foxhole and his brain came to life again—a Japanese soldier had been probing in the inky stillness, looking for an American throat to slit—and had literally stumbled into the foxhole and impaled himself on Kit's upraised blade! Meadows was also now fully awake, and, realizing the situation, stabbed and stabbed until the Nip quit squirming.

The adrenaline was now on high octane for both Kit and Tasker, and they were aware that their position must be known to every enemy soldier sneaking through the tangled brush around them. Weary of war after only a day of its insanity, fatigued into almost a comatose state, Kit realized there would be no more sleep that night. He and Tasker pushed the dead soldier out of their hole, and stared into the blackness until finally the dawn began to make objects visible again.

The Look. Kit began to notice it in the eyes of Meadows, and saw the same thing in Hack and George. It was worst in Walter Horn, the nervous guy from Madison. They had seen the Higgins' boat vaporize just as he had; had watched men fall at the beach, had seen Bennie Friedman lying there dead; had killed enemy soldiers in hand-to-hand fighting. Tasker had been in the foxhole with him when the soldier fell onto Kit's bayonet, and had finished him off as he screamed and squirmed. The Look was a look of dullness, eyes that looked without seeing anything. Nervous exhaustion, lack of sleep, too much tension for too long, fear beyond fear, numbing misery, it all added up quickly to completely overwhelm them. The senses had been engulfed, could only stand so much. Kit wondered; *How did men continue to fight for long periods of time? What gave them the strength to keep on going? War had been this way since the beginning of man, and millions had found themselves dealing with the carnage and raw emotion it inevitably generated. How did they do it? More importantly, how could he keep doing it?* They had only been in battle a few hours, but already there was that look of surpassing indifference, like nobody cared anymore what could happen to them or to anybody else. People just naturally drew inward; survival instinct, Kit figured. *Don't make friends; war is tough enough as it is.* It was good advice. Impossible to keep, of course; but understandable advice given the circumstances.

Kit figured there wasn't a man among them that didn't wish he was moving the other way, toward safety and home, but he guessed it was pride that kept them moving toward the battle. *Death before dishonor.* It was a corny saying, but deep down most guys really believed it, Kit surmised. The terrors of battle bring the reality that you aren't Superman, that death and wounds and trauma can happen to anyone and will eventually happen to you. But the thought that you might not do your duty, that others were depending on you, that thought kept most of them at it until they were dead or carried off the field of battle. Kit realized that it wasn't fighting for his country that kept them going. That was too nebulous a concept. And it wasn't even fighting for those you loved back home. Sure, he wanted them to be proud of him, wanted to protect them. But now they were too far away. What really kept Kit from going completely nuts was the thought that he had to somehow help keep his buddies alive. His world had contracted until they seemed to be what was most important. Daniels would live, but he wasn't here. He was back where he could be patched up and maybe even sent home. Bennie was gone and buried. But Tasker, Hack, George, little Walter, even Lieutenant Sheets, they were worth fighting for, worth killing someone else for, worth protecting with his own life if necessary.

Kit remembered the haunting words of Colonel Danvers at the end of their Pendleton training: "You are going to be afraid in combat. A lot of you are probably afraid you'll be so afraid that you won't be able to do your job. I've tried to prepare you to do your job regardless of how afraid you are. And just keep this in mind. You aren't alone in being afraid. Everybody's afraid…Some of you are going to die in this war. When you joined up nobody promised you that you would ever get to come home again. But there's no use crying about it. I wish you all the best of luck, and maybe you'll live long enough for me to see you again someday."

After surviving the first few hours of bloodshed, Kit understood as never before the awful aftermath of living through hostilities, still in one piece, with more fighting ahead. Bennie really never knew what hit him, and he was where the war couldn't touch him anymore. Kit now knew without question that he could shoot and bayonet to kill, knew that he could charge the enemy despite the fear, knew what it was to watch comrades fall wounded or dead, and knew the terrible price men had to pay to preserve freedom, knew what it meant to want to be one of the ones who made it back to family and friends. He was grateful he had overcome his fears to do his duty. But he was afraid of one more thing—he knew what it was to lose close companions, and what it was to fear losing more of them before it was over.

Chapter 13: Rough Landing

Three months had gone by, and Tank had successfully taken his own crew on twenty missions. Fred Dixon was a fine navigator, and Tank thought often about how happy he was that Dixon and he had been assigned together. They had known each other since the earliest days of NAVCAD training. It sure was nice to have a friend around. John Hamilton was the crew's bombardier, a classy guy from Milwaukee, Wisconsin. Peachy Monroe, the co-pilot, was from Georgia, sporting a nickname of obvious origin. Gunners Mitch Gordon, Leonard Fletcher, and Gerald Washington hailed from Nevada, Tennessee, and Delaware, respectively. *I've got a crew from just about everywhere, sure enough,* thought Tank. But they were his guys, and it hadn't taken many missions for them to gel. Each man was good at his job, and easy to work with. It was a good thing too. Tank had other things to worry about.

Tank remembered what Slim Connors had said about flak, how you get used to it and there was nothing you could do about it anyway, and he found it to be true…somewhat. His plane was hard enough to control without it bouncing around the sky like a pogo stick because of the concussions created by the exploding shells, and he never really got used to the shards of metal making his plane look like a piece of Swiss cheese. There were times he examined the craft after they had landed and he wondered how none of them had suffered serious injury. There seemed to be holes everywhere.

His plane had sustained severe damage several times, but the mechanics just patched it back together and sent him off flying again. Fletcher, one of his waist gunners, had sustained a broken arm that bled badly from getting hit by a piece of flak, but Gordon and Washington had stopped the bleeding and Fletcher was treated once they returned to base. Now on his twenty-first operation with his crew, including a replacement waist gunner, Tank felt good about surviving the war and going home proudly having done his part for freedom. The good feeling didn't last very long on this particular flight.

He remembered learning about the B-24 that even though it had four engines, the loss of any one of them was a serious thing. His team had once again successfully reached their target and released their payload when one of the engines coughed, sputtered, and quit. Tank didn't know if it had been hit with ack-ack or what the exact problem was, but the plane became hard to manage almost immediately.

He wheeled right, out south and west toward the Bay of Bengal, for a couple of reasons. The mountainous jungles below were held by the enemy, and he didn't relish the idea of his crew becoming slave workers on the Japanese railway of death. He also knew that no matter how hard it would be to land his plane on the ocean, it would be a heap sight better than trying to land it in a jungle. There were trees everywhere and no roads he could see that would serve as a temporary landing strip. Maybe they'd get lucky and he could coax the big ship back to the base with three engines.

They weren't lucky. The plane was giving Tank all kinds of fits, and he felt like he was wrestling with a grizzly bear to try to get it to respond correctly. He dropped in elevation and got on the intercom to tell everyone to get ready to ditch in the water. He also instructed Peachy to get word to the base that they weren't going to make it back, and to give them their latitude and longitude so they could send out word to a rescue ship. He had always prided himself on his ability to handle the "Flying Boxcar", but he remembered how pilots had said the B-17 didn't sink when it did an ocean flop. Of course he wasn't flying a B-17, and it wasn't very comforting to know that his B-24 wouldn't float for very long; that is, if it didn't break all to pieces when they hit the water and it didn't float at all.

Everyone prepared for the watery landing, and made sure they could get to the life rafts quickly and get out of the doors as fast as possible. Nobody wanted to get sucked into the depths to become fish food as their plane sank out of sight. There was very little actual training on making a water landing, for obvious reasons, and Tank had never done one before, but he did remember that it was best to land parallel to the wave motion instead of across the waves. Fortunately for them all, they were landing in the Pacific instead of the Atlantic, and the waves were not terribly high. Everyone braced for impact, and Tank leveled the wings as best he could while coming in at a very shallow angle to minimize the shock of hitting the water.

It was awesome and overwhelming to see the water coming up on them so quickly and inexorably. When they hit, one wing caught on a swell, which rotated the plane about a hundred and fifty degrees and damaged the nose. The tail section completely broke off, and seawater began to enter the plane in torrents. Thankfully the crew had already prepared for landing by donning their life jackets after stripping off the extra layers of clothing keeping them warm at high altitude, and they efficiently and rapidly got the rafts outside the ship and inflated them. Almost miraculously nobody was severely injured, although they had all been shaken up quite a bit. All nine members of the crew were able to get into the two rafts and they began to row away from the plane. Their biggest immediate fear was being sucked under the water by the sinking plane. Wet, but thankfully not too cold because of the climate and warm Pacific waters, five men in one raft and four in the other, they assessed their situation.

The rafts were pre-loaded with emergency high-energy chocolate bars and water bottles, and several of the crew had the forethought to bring along extra water and two parachutes so they could cover themselves from the glare of the tropical sun. Nobody knew how long they'd be afloat. Co-pilot Monroe had sent out a Mayday signal as soon as Tank made the decision to ditch the plane, and they were in hopes that the U.S. Navy would send a ship quickly to find them. *All-in-all, a remarkably professional and safe landing,* thought Tank. *Maybe this won't be such a bad experience after all.*

Then again, maybe it would. The plane sank quickly; they estimated less than ten minutes after the crash landing. "It's not only a Flying Coffin, it's a Sinking Coffin too," Dixon said sarcastically.

"But it's not a real coffin, thank God," said Tank. "Nobody bought it, we're all alive, and we're still together." Tank had three of the men in his raft: Dixon, Hamilton, and Gordon. The rest were with Peachy Monroe.

They were all grateful, but a few hours of floating brought a new worry. As if alerted by the crash, sharks began to gather and swim around the rafts. Besides claustrophobia, this was Tank's biggest fear, being in the drink with these monsters. Ever since he had been a boy, he had been alternately thrilled and petrified by stories of the sea. He had especially been fascinated by shark stories. How he had enjoyed those stories as a boy! But he had enjoyed them from afar, nowhere near the sea, and now he was up close and personal with the real creatures, trying very hard to maintain his composure as the leader of the crew while at the same time keeping his knees from knocking against one another.

Some of the crew actually seemed to enjoy the sharks' presence. They laughed and kept trying to hit the beasts with their oars. All Tank could think was how very little rubber there was between himself and the teeth of those large predators. Nearly all of them were bigger than any of the crew, and one seemed longer than the raft they were sitting in. *Where are those Navy boys!? I sure hope they are on their way!*

Chapter 14: Herb Sees Action

Landlubbers have a natural aversion to the ocean. Its enormity, its mysteries, its monsters, and its storms are all fearful unknowns that they instinctively dread. But Herb, like all men raised on the coasts of the world's oceans, was born to it. He had spent thousands of hours sailing, swimming and diving in the saltwater, and saw the sea as a friend rather than an enemy. It was home to him.

He was understandably proud of his ability to take a small boat onto the water and keep it afloat no matter what nature threw at him, and in the stormy North Atlantic he had seen a lot thrown at him in his young life. It was a bit different now that he was a passenger on a huge warship, and when the storm came that afternoon he hoped that the skipper was as good at keeping this giant vessel afloat as he was keeping his little craft safe. When the typhoon struck the ship rolled and tossed, but the helmsman held her steady, and Herb was pleased with her performance. Forty-five minutes later all was well. He had a lot of seasick buddies, but the ship and the helmsman had acquitted themselves well.

Shortly afterward the claxon rang loudly: battle stations! The *Edwards* was not traveling alone. She was part of a convoy of five ships, and the *Vincent*, the ship closest to *Edwards*, had been fired on by a Japanese sub. Herb noticed that at least one of the torpedoes had struck home, and the

Edwards steamed to her rescue. The *Vincent* had indeed taken a shot, but the hole wasn't excessively large, and her pumps were able to handle the inrush of water. She was crippled a bit, but still moving along okay.

So Captain Frederickson went hunting for the submerged submarine that had dared to attack his sister ship. That was the reason the *Edwards* was here, after all. They were here to sink subs. Herb and his fellow crewmen were ordered to prepare depth charges and set them to detonate at a hundred feet. They had practiced this skill many times, but it was Herb's first chance to send the charges after a real enemy sub. Five of the cans were consecutively tossed off the aft deck of the *Edwards*, and after sinking to the required depth they detonated one by one. The concussions and ensuing waterspouts were impressive, to say the least. Herb couldn't help but think of the enemy sailors in that sub, waiting anxiously to see if one of the explosions split her seams and allowed the big ocean to pour in. Sometimes a sub could completely break apart, in which case all the men would quickly drown. But more often leaks would form, and when they were serious enough so much water entered that the sub sank to her doom. He thought about his own ship breaking apart, but knew that at least he and his fellow sailors had a chance if that happened. For a submarine a hundred feet or so beneath the surface, when too much water came in there was absolutely no hope. *Right now I can't think of a good way to die,* mused Herb, *but dying that way, slowly suffocating, what a horrible way to go.*

It made Herb think of the beginning and ending of the lamenting poem of Elizabeth Barrett Browning called *If Thou Must Love Me…*

If thou must love me, let it be for nought except love's sake only…

Love me for love's sake, that evermore thou mayst love on, through love's eternity.

How sad to love one doomed to die a horrible death. It was a bit comforting to think of a love that was eternal, a love that only loved for love's sake, and not for what another could do for it. *But only God's love is truly like that,* thought Herb. *We mortals attempt it, but so often fail.*

After an hour or so of searching for the submarine's motion or some evidence that she was destroyed, the captain finally called off the attack. *Either she has gone to the bottom or gone out of range and they had lost her.* The convoy resumed its original course and formation.

Topside and off-duty for now, Herb strolled the deck and breathed in the salty air, enjoying the balmy weather, musing about how his mother and father and Karen were doing and what they would think if they could see him now, when Lieutenant Dawson called all topside hands aft for an important announcement.

"The CO just informed me that we've received a communiqué to let us know of a downed bomber in the Bay of Bengal within a hundred miles of our position. We're changing course to go to her rescue, to see if any of her crew have survived. Apparently there was some foul-up in communications, and we're just now being notified even though the bomber crashed over forty hours ago. We want to alert all of you to keep a weather eye out for any life rafts, especially as we approach the vicinity of the crash. It's a big ocean, gentlemen, but we don't want our flyboys to think we can't find the needle in the haystack. Get back to your stations, but if you are free, or are stationed topside, look like you've never looked before, and report anything that might look like it belongs to us. That is all."

Herb noticed Ollie and Virgil near the rail, and when they were dismissed he went over to talk to them. "Boy, he's right about it being a big ocean," Ollie said. "Think we can find them?" Virgil offered, "I'm sure they're praying from their end. Let's pray from our end too, and the good Lord will help us. I believe that." Herb was reminded again why he liked the Oklahoman. *Such simple faith. God surely would honor that. Maybe here was a man who could actually love just for love's sake.*

Chapter 15: Choppy Seas

Tank was the leader in one raft, Peachy Monroe the leader in the other. At first they attached the rafts together so they wouldn't drift apart during the night, but when the swells became too large both rafts began to take on more water and created fears in the men that each raft's motion could possibly swamp the other, so they separated the rafts again and trusted that they wouldn't get too far away from each other.

After conferring, Hogan and Monroe felt the best thing to do was to try to strike land as soon as possible. They estimated they were less than fifty miles from the coast of Burma, and although the Japanese presence there was thick, they believed they could land unnoticed at night, make their way through the jungle and return to base without being captured. Tank was glad they had done all those exercises in the "jungle" back home. He felt he and his men could survive for days if they had to do it. Escaping the Japanese patrols might be another matter, but reaching land and getting out of this water was far more preferable to him than floating endlessly hoping the navy boys would find them, with dwindling supplies and sharks for company.

All had been going smoothly for many hours now. The ocean was calm, the weather sticky and warm but not terribly hot. The parachute material made perfect shade from the sun, and they still had sufficient supplies of water for several more days. Hopefully the U.S. Navy would discover their whereabouts or they would make landfall within forty-eight hours. The rafts had compasses, and they figured their best bet was to row north. Surely it would take no more than two days to reach *terra firma* again.

The serenity and ease of the airmen was broken by the rather sudden appearance of clouds to their southwest. They had heard of the monsoon season of India and Southeast Asia, but so far they had not experienced it. That was about to change, and give them an experience they would never forget. The winds began to pick up dramatically, and the ocean swells rise accordingly. They were glad at this point they had separated the rafts, because the increased wave heights were playing havoc with their boats anyway, and the thought of the problems they would create for each other if they were tied together was enough to make them shudder. Men from both rafts were beginning to bail water as the intensity of the winds built and the waves began to break over their gunwales.

And then the rains came. Tank had seen "gully washers" in his days on the plains, where it rained cats and dogs, where three or even four inches of rain could fall in an hour, with a sudden stop as though a faucet handle had been turned, but he never dreamed the heavens could drop water like this. The water came in torrents, in buckets, as though some irate sky giant was emptying his bathtub on them all at once, endeavoring to drown them and send them down the drain. The rain came so hard it was almost impossible to see the other men in the raft, even though they were just a few feet away. To see the other raft fifty or more yards away was of course totally impossible. The men bailed and bailed, lost in a world to themselves, isolated from everyone and everything else in the universe. It was even hard to breathe, the rain was so thick. The men wondered if you could drown from rain. Tank, from an arid country town where the inhabitants constantly prayed for rain, wished his fellow Texans could see this. All he could pray now was, "Lord, make it STOP!" It seemed like it had rained for hours, that Tank's prayer would never be answered, but after forty-five minutes or so of torrential downpour the heavens relented and the system moved on toward Burma and Thailand.

Now it was time to assess. As the atmosphere cleared a bit Tank and his crew began to search for the other raft, but they could see nothing except the storm system rolling inexorably northeast and the ocean beginning to calm a bit as the storm passed. They did realize that the winds had been pushing them toward land, and for that they were grateful. Maybe they'd reach landfall by early morning now.Meanwhile, Tank had no idea where the second raft had gone. He had put Peachy Monroe in that raft on purpose since he was the co-pilot, and he knew Monroe was a competent leader with a good head on his shoulders. He couldn't worry too much about that now anyway, because he and the men on his raft, having survived the storm and refilled all their containers with water, were reunited with their squadron of sharks. The men weren't thirsty anymore, but they knew if they didn't get some food they'd begin to be seriously hungry. It had been almost two full days since the crash, and they were going to run out of food before long. None of them knew how many hours, or days, they'd have to float and hope for rescue. Dixon offered that maybe they could catch one of the small sharks for food. Tank thought this was a bunch of nonsense, but several others thought the idea worth trying out.

They looked hard, and finally spotted a "tiny" one between four and five feet long. "What can we use for a hook, and what can we use for bait?" Ever resourceful, they found a piece of metal in the parachute harness that could be bent to form the hook, and of course they had more than enough line from the parachute itself to play out the hook into the water. They ran a piece of colored cloth through the hook, and tried to entice the beast to bite. It didn't take too long to realize that, although the beast nosed the hook a time or two, it wasn't going to take a bite. *Why was it that sharks wanted to bite when you didn't want them to, and refused to bite when it was to your advantage?* Like fishermen from all of history, they finally gave up in disgust.

There was nothing they could do about the other raft except to launch a flare and perhaps Monroe's raft could see it and return signal so they could be reunited. The rafts were equipped with flare guns and several flares, so Gordon, the waist gunner, shot one red meteor flare into the sky as the others scanned the horizon to see if there might be an answering flare released by the other raft.

In this hope they were disappointed, but something else happened shortly that proved the Lord's providence over their journey. As they vainly watched for a return flare signal from their buddies, Dixon noticed to starboard the aerial and smokestacks of a large ship, and it seemed to be heading their way! The men were understandably excited, yet fearful too. The ship could be their navy friends looking for them, or it could be the Imperial Japanese Navy out for blood. Either way, they were helpless. They couldn't run anywhere even if they needed to, they had no weapons with which to fight, and they had no cover if the Japs started shooting. All they could do was wait—in hope and dread—and see their fate unfold.

They didn't have to wait long. Within minutes the ship grew bigger in their field of view, their apprehension dissipating as they realized it was an Allied vessel instead of the enemy. Minutes more brought the monstrous craft near, and they could see *Edwards* painted on her side. A smaller boat was lowered and manned by sailors, and began to move toward the raft. Tank, Dixon, Gordon, and Hamilton were all smiles, and those smiles were returned by the party sent to pick them up. Pulling up alongside, a grinning sailor said in a New England accent, "Ahoy there commander! We noticed your flare, and Captain Frederickson of the U.S.S. *Edwards* requests your presence aboard his ship if you don't have another pressing engagement."

Tank responded to the invitation with elation. "It would do us a great honor to join your captain on board his worthy vessel. We at this present time have no other urgent business to conduct. To whom do I have the pleasure of speaking sir?"

"Ensign Herbert Johnson, at your service, sir. Would you men be so kind as to quit your vessel and join us on the cutter for transport to our warship?"

Chapter 16: A Diehard Enemy

Lieutenant Sheets gathered his squad and told them that he was extremely proud of them for driving the Japanese back from their strongholds. They were into the second week of battle on New Guinea, and slowly they had punched a salient into the Japanese line. Kit, Tasker, Hack, and George were eating their rations and discussing the enemy they had come so far from home to face.

"It's hard to conquer these people; they think they're the *shido minzoku*, the chosen people."

"Yeah, fanatics like this are the worst kind of enemy. They are taught from the cradle to die for the emperor."

"I hear most of the Japanese haven't ever even seen Emperor Hirohito, or heard him speak. I don't understand why they think he's some kind of god."

"Yeah, no fireside chats with him, huh?"

"Well, it don't seem to make no difference with them. They seem willing enough to kill…or die…in his name."

"You won't catch me on one of those banzai charges or kamikaze flights. Those guys are plain nuts!"

"Yeah, I sure don't want to be no POW, but I reckon it beats running straight into certain death. I'll let them take the honorable way out, but I'm going to do all I can to keep my hide intact and get back to the folks."

Kit realized the differences between the Japanese way of life and the philosophies of most Americans were so vast that there could be no coming together in agreement. They had heard through the grapevine that the Japanese were the most tenacious fighters on the planet, mainly because they didn't have a whole lot of choice. Their superiors seemed to have only two options available: conquer or die trying. It seemed as though the Americans were motivated by being pulled from the front, so to speak. They fought because of some noble idea of protecting the homeland or keeping freedom alive or saving their buddies. Their motivations were invisible and nebulous. Kit was sure the Japs also wanted to protect their homeland, but part of what made them so aggressive in bringing war to others was the push they had from behind. If an American officer beat a boot or abused him to extreme it would mean a court-martial. For a Japanese officer it was expected that they take out their rage on their inferiors, and beat them as much as necessary to cause them to fight and die. *The cultural divide was just too great to bridge*, he thought. *We can't understand them, and they sure can't understand us.*

Tasker, who had been taught the history of war by his father from his childhood, talked about the wisdom in retreat and counterattack. For the Japanese it seemed there was never retreat. Kit had heard of their *Bushido* code and their willingness to die rather than surrender. He felt they had taken an extreme view, but he realized that there was something to be admired in their willingness to give everything for their cause, even if he couldn't really understand or approve of their cause.

War is hard. It's even harder when your enemy never believes in giving up or giving in. As the war progressed, Kit and his companions were going to pay a high price for this cultural divide. The Japanese thought only cowards surrendered. How would they treat men who didn't fight until the end once they had them in their power?

Chapter 17: Capture

The orders took Kit, Tasker, Hack, and the others by surprise. Lieutenant Sheets met with his men at 0800 and told them that they were moving back to the coast, to be transported to their north and west to engage in a new offensive.

"But we've been pushing the Japs back here effectively for the last couple of weeks, helping the British reclaim New Guinea. Why move on now?" Tasker, always ready with an argument, couldn't understand the thinking of the bigwigs, and didn't mind saying so. Sheets had his theory ready for that question. "Look, you're right. But you know when General Wainwright surrendered the Philippines to the enemy that "Dugout Doug" MacArthur and the whole U.S. Army looked like incompetent fools, and they've been itching to rectify the situation and free our men who are rotting in POW camps in the northern part of the country. Well, the generals finally have a plan for retaking the Philippines, and it will start in the southern part of the archipelago. The plan as I understand it is to concentrate on fighting to regain Mindanao, since Japanese presence there is smaller than on Luzon to the north. Once we've established ourselves there, we push toward Manila. My guess is we get to be in the first wave, since we now have experience at storming beaches and jungle fighting."

All this made sense to Kit, and in one way he knew it was an honor to be picked for the job. On the other hand, they had reached some success here on New Guinea, had endured and overcome and to some degree had accustomed themselves to this place and their role in the war, and he didn't relish another beach assault and an unknown situation. But what was it Danvers had drilled into them at boot? *Nothing matters so little as a soldier's personal preference. Nobody ever asked what you wanted to do. They just told you what to do, and you did it for the team.*

So twenty-four hours later they were heading toward the Philippine Islands on a troop transport along with a thousand other Marines. At least for the moment they were out of the jungle and safe, unless a Japanese sub got the notion to put a tin fish into their side. Kit tried to keep that idea out of his head. It was a hassle, and took awhile, but the officers set up some showers for the Marines, who hadn't changed clothes in more than two weeks, and were covered in grime, sweat, and blood. Oh just to feel clean again! It was incredible how it helped one's attitude. And the food was better on board too…much better than they had while jungle fighting, where cold canned rations was the norm. Maybe this wasn't going to be such a bad deal after all—until they had to face dug-in positions on the next beach, that is. One thing Kit had learned though: soldiers learned to adapt quickly to situations, and they learned to enjoy any fairly pleasant moments and put future terrible moments out of their minds for the time being. *Who knew what was going to happen tomorrow anyway?*

For three days the sailing was uneventful. The Marines were now clean, well-fed, and rested. Kit took the time to write a letter home, and to get to know his mates a bit better. He found out that Hack Wilson wanted to be a dentist when the war ended—had always been fascinated by teeth. "I'm not sure you have a good name for a dentist," Kit remarked. "I'd think twice about letting a guy named Hack stick his fingers in my mouth and start banging around." Wilson chuckled, "Oh, I aim to go by Henry James when I put out my shingle. Henry James Wilson has a nice professional ring to it, don't you think? I'm sure customers will flock to my office."

Kit tried again to reach out to Walter Horn, the tiny Marine from Wisconsin. The trauma of battle had faded somewhat from most of the Marines, at least outwardly, now that they were away from it for a few days, but little Walter was withdrawn and had lines of worry etched on his face. Kit hadn't seen him smile the whole time they'd been aboard ship. After his interesting conversation with Hack, Kit thought maybe talking about the future would draw Horn out a bit and give him something positive to think about. "Walter, what do you want to do when you get back home after the war?" Kit's ploy backfired as Walter responded, "I don't think I'll ever see home again." Anderson was taken aback and tried to press the matter. "Come on, Walter, most of us are going to survive this war and start our lives all over again. Surely you'll be one of the guys who make it."

"I don't think so", Horn insisted. "I can't seem to shake the feeling that the next battle will be my last. I'm just trying to get used to the idea."

Nothing Kit could say or do seemed to make a dent in Walter's depressing thoughts. His attitude weighed on Kit. He figured the surest way to buy the farm was to assume it was your fate and not do everything in your power to make sure it didn't happen. The ship was drawing near Mindanao, and Kit realized that their time of ease was coming to an end. It came much sooner than he expected.

The Japanese air force had experienced much success at the start of the war. Their use of aircraft was superb in the bombing raid on Pearl Harbor, and they had fought with skill in other Pacific theaters. But the U.S. Navy air force had responded beautifully, albeit slowly. By this time in the war the Allies were beginning to win air battles and decimate the Zeroes that had been such a thorn in their side for months. That thought didn't particularly help on this day, however, when a dozen Japanese fighter planes appeared on the northern horizon and began to swoop down on the troop transport carrying the Marines, who found themselves with no air cover.

The Navy men sprang into action just like they'd been trained, and Kit was impressed with the discipline of the sailors as they manned their anti-aircraft guns and began to hammer away at the Jap pilots, who were buzzing around them like angry hornets ready to sting. Their transport had both Oerlikon twenty millimeter cannons and twin Bofors forty millimeter guns, and those babies could really sing. Everyone topside was looking for a place to hide from the strafing bullets coming from the enemy fighters, and the cacophony of sound was deafening. Kit, Tasker, Hack, and Walter all happened to be together in the forward part of the ship when the attacking Zeroes first appeared, and they huddled together near a bulkhead, trying to be as small a target as possible. They figured that running around on deck trying to find a way to get below held greater risk than staying put behind some thick metal.

Because they were on deck they had a beautiful, if horrifying, view of the decisive next few moments. The Bofors guns had struck one of the Japanese planes and given it a fatal wound. Smoke streamed from the enemy flier's craft and it began to lose altitude rapidly. The Marines were excited to see it crash land into the blue ocean, but the Japanese pilot decided that as long as he wasn't going home to Nippon, he'd at least take some Allies to a watery grave too. He stabilized his descent enough to aim his plane toward the ship, and with horror the Marines saw that he was going to ram them. Exploding with the force of thirty detonating torpedoes the Japanese plane hit the troop transport, and over a thousand sailors and Marines died instantly because the Marine quarters were located here and many of the men were below decks. The crash virtually split the transport in two, and she wasn't going to stay afloat long. Fortunately for the awed Marines on deck, they had obeyed orders to wear their life vests at all times while topside. Unfortunately, they had almost none of their belongings and didn't know what to do next. A sailor appeared and told them to help him get a lifeboat into the water, and they wasted no time in following that order. The chaos aboard was incredible, but their sailor friend remained fairly calm and gave them simple directions, and amazingly within minutes their boat was on the water and they were in it. Anti-aircraft fire from the other transports in the convoy downed several Zeroes, and the rest of the Japanese fighters turned away to find less defended prey, so at least the surviving Marines and sailor didn't have to worry about being strafed while in the small lifeboat. Unfortunately, the rest of the U.S. ships were heading onward toward their pre-arranged destination. Surely they had seen the troop transport hit by the plane, but inexplicably they did not tarry to look for survivors. Perhaps they were wary of searching for fear that submarines would attack.

Kit and friends had launched the lifeboat and were afloat none too soon, for the ship was going down fast. It had been less than ten minutes since the explosion but they saw that she would be under water in only a couple more minutes. They rowed with a will to pull away from the stricken vessel, and watched with dread as she sank out of sight. They tried to spot Lieutenant Sheets or another boat, but failed to see him or anything else except the retreating ships from their convoy. Tasker said, "I'm afraid Sheets was below taking a nap when this all started. Maybe it was a nap he never woke up from." Kit feared as much. He realized it had been a miracle that he and his best friends had survived. *Now what to do? They were on their own.*

Thankfully their sailor friend, who identified himself as yeoman Doug Richards, took charge, and knew what resources were contained in the lifeboat. "Look, our position was due east of northern Borneo and south/southwest of Mindanao when we were attacked. We are within forty miles of both those islands at present. Unfortunately for us the Japs hold them both. My recommendation is that we head west by northwest into the South China Sea and skirt Borneo. The Japanese have ships and subs in that area, but so do we. Hopefully it's at least a fifty-fifty chance we run into our guys out there instead of theirs. Making landfall anywhere near here almost guarantees our capture...and possible execution."

The Marines didn't have a better plan, so Richards found the boat's compass, became honorary captain and navigator, and assigned Hack as the quartermaster to organize their food and water resources. After thirty minutes of searching and thinking, Hack said "We've probably got enough food for a week if we are careful, and water for maybe fourteen days. This boat was meant for sixteen people, and there are only five of us."

"Fine", said Richards, "Anderson and Horn will take the first shift on the oars, I'll man the tiller, and we'll rotate at oars every thirty minutes. I think there's a current at the northern tip of Borneo that bears off to the west, and if we hit it we won't have to work so hard at rowing."

Kit began to pull on the oar, a new experience for him. Being a mountain man he had never thought about being a sailor, that's for sure. He glanced every once in a while at Walter, and tried a bit to cheer him up, but Walter, instead of being thankful and excited to still be alive, seemed even more indifferent about his fate, assuming it had gone from bad to worse, and determined to believe he wouldn't ever see home again.

Nightfall came, and Richards calculated they were now directly east of Borneo's northern shore. He knew the Japanese still held the island in a firm grip, but he actually had no information about the number of troops there or how many ships normally plied these waters. He hoped that most of the Japanese Navy was kept busy far away to the northeast, fighting fellow Americans in other war theaters, and that the Japanese on Borneo were apathetic and lazy, and wouldn't be looking too hard for Allied troops floating in a small lifeboat.

Richards told everyone to rest easy during the night, and he would stay at the tiller for as long as possible, watching the compass carefully to make sure they stayed on course. He told Kit he would wake him if he became too drowsy, and allow him to steer. He knew they wouldn't move far anyway during the darkness without the oars. Exhausted, Kit fell asleep almost immediately, but was shaken awake about 0400 by the sailor. *"Sorry, old man, I can't seem to keep my eyes open. You'll have to man the helm for a bit."* Kit was actually excited to get to steer the little boat for a few hours; again, a new experience for him. He was careful to keep his eye on the compass and not let the boat move to the west. Borneo wasn't too far away according to Richards and they wanted to be well north of it before they moved back to the west and hopefully, toward friendly waters.

As it became light they resumed their rowing schedule, and sure enough, north of the big island they hit a westerly current that moved them along at a good pace. Richards insisted that they continue to row as well, because he wanted to leave Borneo behind. He knew that the Japanese used it as a base of operations, and that there would be boats and planes leaving the island periodically throughout the day.

It was just such a patrol that found them about 0930. The boat wasn't particularly large, similar in size to a U.S. Coastguard cutter, but it was much larger than their vessel, and what was far worse, it was equipped with machine guns. They spotted the enemy vessel a few minutes before it pulled up, and Richards told everyone, "When she draws alongside just hold your horses. We are sitting ducks and totally at the mercy—if there is any—of the Japs. If they decide to gun us down I'm afraid there is nothing we can do anyway. Let's just be as quiet and cooperative as possible and pray like crazy that they are in a good mood today."

Marines by nature are fighters, and this advice grated against that nature now, but Kit, Tasker, and Hack were in no shape to argue, and Walter had obviously given up hope long ago. They had no weapons except the personal pocket knives that were part of their uniforms. All their guns and ammo had been stowed away when their ship was attacked, and they were now exposed and vulnerable. There was literally no place to hide. Hack said, "This is worse than storming a beach. At least there we had some guns and ammo and could shoot back." Kit thought of the twenty-third Psalm, about the part that says *"Yea, though I walk through the valley of the shadow of death, I will fear no evil; For Thou art with me; Thy rod and Thy staff they comfort me..."*

126

How did King David feel no fear, he wondered? Kit was reassured by the verse, but had to confess that there was still some fear at the thought of being gunned down without having a chance to fight back.

There wasn't much time to meditate, however. The Japanese pulled up within a couple of minutes, leveled their guns at the Americans, and seemed ready to fire away. Kit thought he had never seen such remorseless faces. They had surely seen much death in their young lives, as he had, so what was a little more to them? All it would take would be one order from their superior, or one little spark to ignite them, and the soldiers would commence firing.

The man who was their obvious leader couldn't speak English, but his menacing body language communicated clearly that if the Americans gave them any trouble, he would not hesitate to quickly remove them from the land of the living. By motions he ordered them to toss their line to one of his men so the boat could be tied to his vessel. This was done, they clambered aboard the Japanese craft and were promptly searched, relieved of their wallets, watches, and pocket knives, and then had their hands tied behind their backs. The Nips were none too gentle in the tying of the knots, and Kit's wrists were chafed and pinched by the ropes. Roughly tossed into a small room below and guarded by one of the Japanese sailors, the patrol boat triumphantly returned to base.

Once ashore they were led to a large compound where they were confined in a small room, and by signs told to remain still. Their hands remained tied behind their backs and again, a guard stayed in the room with them. *They must think we're real dangerous men,* thought Kit. *Exactly how we could cause them problems or escape, however, is beyond me. We have no weapons, and wouldn't even know where to go if we got out of this joint.*

Thankfully they were fed after a couple of hours, even if it was just a thin gruel that Kit would have roundly rejected if he was back at home. But this definitely wasn't home, and he drank it all, not knowing when the next meal would come. With their hands still bound they had to be fed by the guard, who poured the repulsive mixture down their throats rapidly, causing them to choke more than once. This seemed to delight the guard, who cackled at their misfortunes. Their minds were burning to know what their future would be, but nobody visited them except a new guard being posted after a number of hours, so they attempted to sleep, uncomfortable and still not sure if they were to be summarily killed or kept for slave labor.

The next morning they found out. A Captain Toma entered their room and introduced himself. "Are you Americans, British, or Australian?" His English was very good, and when Tasker mentioned this to him he said he had grown up in a bilingual home and also studied at Oxford.

Richards, still assuming command as captain of the disheveled group, told Toma they were Americans, but that all they were required to tell him by the Geneva Convention was their name, rank, and serial number. Toma brushed this aside quickly. "I do not care about military information from you. You are simply valuable to my people because you are young and strong and will be able to work hard on a special project in which we are engaged. I speak of the rail line we are building between Bangkok and Rangoon. The project proceeds well, but many of our workers grow weak in the jungles and need to be replaced. My superiors will be excited to see I have found additional help for them."

Tasker, despite his lack of a bargaining chip, said, "What if we don't want to work on your special project?" Toma, in a good humor, smiled and ignored the sarcasm inherent in the query, and responded, "Well, soldier, I hope you want to work. It is the only reason I have kept you alive, and it is the only way for you to stay alive in the coming months. All of you will leave for Thailand and Camp Changi this afternoon with the other prisoners we have captured."

Chapter 18: In the Drink...Again!

The *Edwards* had returned to the convoy with her rescued airmen, and held the north flank. She had been assigned as part of an escort for several freighters and tankers to protect them from Jap subs, and she churned along keeping a sharp lookout for the enemy. The Bay of Bengal was swarming with Japanese, but also with American ships and submarines. You could run into anybody anywhere out here. Tank, Gordon, and Hamilton were on deck enjoying the sights and sounds of a new world for them. Dixon was off checking out the workings of the ship aft somewhere. Herb had introduced Fred to Ollie and Virgil, and let Virgil know that Dixon was a fellow Oklahoman. They were excited to meet each other and became quick friends, both of them ganging up good-naturedly on Ollie the Alabaman. Kidding aside, the southerners had a lot in common, and they enjoyed telling stories of their experiences growing up in rural America below the Mason-Dixon line.

Meanwhile, Tank and company were commenting on their adventures as fliers, then as floaters, and now as shipmates.

"My kids will never believe all this when I tell them in twenty years about my war experiences", said Gordon.

"You don't even have kids yet, but my wife had a baby two months ago, so I've got to get home to that one I haven't even met," piped in Hamilton.

"I didn't even leave a girl behind," said Tank. "But when I get home and find one, I'll have stories to tell that will amaze her. Speaking of being amazed, I can't get over how different it is here compared to being back at the air base. I wonder what that doohickie over there is for?"

At that moment Herb came walking by. He stopped to chat a moment with the three flyboys, and asked, "Doohickie? What in the world are you talking about?" Tank grinned and added, "A doohickie is a thing that you don't know what it is. Don't you Harvard boys understand English?"

"English, yes, Southern, no." Herb was grinning too, and shaking his head at the differences between America's great regions. Herb said, "Okay. So far I've learned that we say you guys while Southerners say y'all, we say crayfish while you say crawdads, you like your tea sweet and cold while we like it hot and straight, and when you say "you bet" you mean you agree, but when we say you bet we mean you are making a wager. Oh, and one more thing, we say pop but you call it coke, no matter what kind of soft drink you order!"

Tank grinned and added, "You forgot about fixin' to cut the lights out." Perplexed, Herb threw up his hands, and

Tank explained. "Fixin' to means you are about to do something, and cut out the lights obviously means to turn them off. Only highfalutin' Harvard people haven't heard talk like this before. Are you highfalutin'?"

Herb smiled and said "I haven't the foggiest notion of what you are saying. Highfalutin'?"

"Yeah", Tank said, "it means you're too big for yore britches."

Herb countered, "Up North we just don't talk this way."

Tank finished with, "Well, just remember Ensign Johnson, the word Texas is from an old Spanish word that means 'We don't care how you do it up North.'"

Gordon laughed as Herb gave up and asked, "So how are our passengers from the bomber? Is the U.S. Navy treating you right?"

"Can't complain, Ensign Johnson," responded Tank, "and besides, if the Navy is anything like the Air Force, it wouldn't do much good to complain anyway."

Hamilton, wanting to communicate their gratitude at being plucked out of the water, said, "Hey, you can serve me hard tack and plain water the whole time I'm on board. I'm just glad to be on something bigger and more steady than that little life raft we were floating in a couple of days ago."

"Amen to that," added Tank. "It's a lot nicer having this steel deck and sixty feet of clearance between me and those sharks down there. An inch or less of rubber raft separating me from them sure made me nervous."

Herb laughed, "Well, you're safe now. Sharks and unstable rafts will be the least of your worries for a while. And remember, this is a destroyer, so we look forward to a Jap submarine arriving. It will give us some excitement, and a chance to keep the hunters away from their prizes."

Tank figured he had enough excitement for one week, so he silently prayed for a very uneventful rest of the voyage. With no duties to perform his crew decided to go nap a bit while they had the chance. In a few days they'd be back at the air base, but that meant jumping right back into work and flying more missions over the jungle.

Later that evening, an hour before sunset, Tank and his friends returned topside after their nap and fourth straight card game, bored and ready for something different, and were again leaning on the rail chatting when they noticed a tremendous explosion on the freighter about half a mile away to starboard. Before they could wrap their minds around what was happening a second explosion rocked the doomed ship, and it began to list heavily to port. *What in the world?*

The sailors on the *Edwards* were running to battle stations, with a horn blaring and a loud announcement from their commander. It dawned on Tank that the convoy was under attack, and that torpedoes had already claimed one of the ships. He also realized that the destroyer was now tasked with engaging the sub or subs, and that it might be a good idea for him and his buddies to make sure they had on life jackets and knew where the lifeboats were.

The *Edwards'* crew certainly had been drilled well. They manned their stations quickly and professionally, and the big ship headed for the supposed position of the sub that had sent the two fish into the freighter. *Edwards'* captain surmised the submarine was in the direction of the setting sun. It was a favorite trick of Japanese submarine commanders to attack at this time of day and from that direction because it was harder to spot them looking into the sun's rays.

There was no sign of the sub on the surface, but it had fired from periscope depth and submerged further to run away from the advancing destroyer. Sonar operators from the *Edwards* were picking up a ping giving her location, and now the captain had to guess her depth. "Set depth charges to one hundred feet", he commanded. Dixon and Hamilton were amazed at how the sailors adjusted the charges by setting a hydrostatic valve, prepared them for launch, and then fired them. *Whoooosh*...followed by an explosion after the charges had sunk to the required depth. The way those heavy drums were thrown off the ship demonstrated the power of modern warfare. Each drum weighed between two thousand to three thousand pounds, and they were thrown two-hundred fifty yards from the ship. *How much thrust is required for that kind of toss?* Hamilton, the bombardier, was fascinated with the machinery of war and how it had evolved over the years. Technology was a marvelous thing, alright!

The men of the *Edwards* were so engrossed in chasing the first Japanese sub that they weren't alert to the possibility of a second or third enemy vessel being in the area. The sonar operator noticed two more pinging spots on his instrument panel soon after they engaged the first sub, and informed Captain Frederickson, but he was focused on bringing carnage to the first attacker, and didn't respond as quickly as he normally would. It turned out to be a big mistake.

The Japanese, like the Germans, liked to hunt in wolf-packs. They especially liked to use the technique of launching torpedoes from one submarine to lure destroyers into pursuit, and then firing at the attackers when their backs were turned, so to speak. The strategy worked to perfection this time. From two thousand yards to port a second Jap sub fired three torpedoes at *Edwards*, and they were on the mark. One just missed the big ship to stern, but two of the missiles exploded, one amidships, and one where the depth charges were stored. Several powerful secondary explosions rocked the warship, bowling over sailors and the flyboys like pins. Twenty-four sailors died instantly when the depth charges exploded. Tank, Dixon, Hamilton, and Gordon didn't know what to do. Struggling to their feet they saw with panic that the ship was already heeling over, and that there were several fires raging out of control. Thankfully Herb noticed them and ran to tell them to follow him to the lifeboats, the abandon ship signal loudly drumming in their ears.

The ship was equipped with lifeboats and rafts as well. The ship was listing even further, and it was apparent to even the landlubbers that she was a goner. There wasn't a lot of screaming or yelling, but panic was on the faces of some of the seamen, and that didn't help the flyboys' nerves any. Two lifeboats on the starboard side got off safely, but one had a hole in it and was useless.

Herb led the men to the port side of the ship and discovered that all the lifeboats had been lowered already, but there were rafts available. The bomber crew had obviously not practiced manning life rafts from a sinking destroyer, but they were very good at following orders quickly, and they already had their life vests on and fastened securely. Herb told them to jump into the water and the raft would pick them up. They were a bit dubious about this, since even with the ship leaning over that direction it was still a considerable distance to drop to the water, over forty feet Tank guessed. But the alternative being what it was, they all looked at one another and leaped as far from the destroyer as possible. The ship was sinking, fast, and everyone was swimming or rowing as quickly as they could away from it.

Sure enough, here came Herb in the life raft, in the nick of time, just like the cavalry in the old westerns. Herb, two other seamen, and the four airmen were safely on the raft, which could hold up to ten men. Herb was grateful they were away, with a raft and supplies, but he pondered the fate of his two best friends aboard the *Edwards*, Ollie and Virgil. Had they made it to safety as well?

The *Edwards* was in its death throes, heading for the bottom. Safely away from the sinking vessel, Herb, the senior sailor on the raft, was now a captain with the responsibility of trying to save the lives of his crew. He had always wondered if he would make captain, but this surely wasn't what he had in mind. As they began to organize rowers to get the raft moving toward the mainland, they heard loud yelling from two hundred yards away. Looking in that direction, they noticed flailing hands waving to them and could hear indiscernible shouts. Pulling up to the men in the water, Herb was overjoyed to see both Ollie and Virgil, clinging to floating debris. They pulled the two drenched sailors into the raft, glad to have their companions back.

"Trying to row off and leave us?" Ollie's tongue-in-cheek question was intended to elicit a laugh, and it worked.

"You mates were doing so well with your swimming stroke I didn't think you'd like to join us. We might have slowed you down." Herb was grinning too, the relief evident in his face.

"Well, we didn't want to beat y'all to land; you might have been embarrassed. So we thought we'd join you to show you how to navigate your boat."

Herb, glad that so many had made it off the doomed destroyer alive, was glad to have some more Navy men to help him in the situation, but he was struck again with the responsibility he had, how the lives of the men on the raft depended largely on how he led them. Looking out over the rolling swells of the broad Pacific, he quoted the first stanza of the Navy hymn:

Eternal Father, strong to save,

Whose arms hath bound the restless wave,

Who bidd'st the mighty ocean deep

Its own appointed limits keep;

Oh, hear us when we cry to Thee,

For those in peril on the sea!

Tank thought it sounded beautiful, and he earnestly joined in that prayer of deliverance. He couldn't believe it— here he was, a boy from the panhandle of Texas, growing up hundreds of miles from any saltwater, and this was now the second time in less than ten days that he was floating with the sharks! *What were the odds?*

Tank figured they'd be picked up soon anyway by the ships from the rest of the convoy, but in this he was sorely disappointed. They had sailed on. Why? Herb had to fill him in; it was new Navy policy for captains to have sole discretion on trying to stop and render aid to sinking vessels and her survivors, and some captains chose to save their own ship and men and the bulk of a convoy rather than come to the rescue and be a sitting duck for a torpedo. As they had found out the hard way, it could cost many more lives if a captain was too chivalrous. Tank was thankful that at least this time they were in a larger raft and were accompanied by sailors, but that wasn't a lot of comfort to him. He remembered Slim Connors comment that with flyboys there was no shortage of prayer. Slim had been referring to prayer while flying through flak, but Tank now realized prayer was appropriate all the time. *Nothing like war to keep you on your spiritual toes!*

Ollie said he was worried about being found by the Japanese. He had heard the story of the U.S.S. *Panay*, a Navy gunboat bombed by the Japanese in nineteen thirty-seven, and how enemy planes had continued to strafe the water and kill survivors who were floating on bits of debris. He also knew that a few American skippers had retaliated and killed Japanese survivors floating in the water. *What if the Nips find us and start shooting?! We wouldn't stand a chance.*

Darkness fell, and a storm brewed up. "I can't believe it!" Tank muttered, and shook his head at the Lord's humor. *Going through another cats and dogs downpour in one week.* He had heard of déjà vu, and he certainly experienced it here. It was like someone had recorded his last outing on a raft and decided to play the music again — same song, second verse. Sure enough, the deluge came, and after about an hour it moved on. The Navy men didn't seem too uptight about it, which helped calm him some. And so far, no sharks had arrived.

The next morning they scanned the horizon and realized they had lost sight of the other Americans on the water. It didn't necessarily mean the other rafts and lifeboats were many miles away. Without binoculars or a telescope you couldn't make out small vessels unless they were within seven miles or so. Still, it was a big ocean, and seemed bigger because it seemed no one else was on it. The good news was that they had plenty of supplies for several days, they were fairly close to land, and the water was calm and manageable. They would come up with a good plan for getting back where they belonged. The bad news, as it turned out, was that they didn't have time to implement a plan, because they saw the smokestack of a Japanese troop transport to their south, and in less than an hour they were aboard, prisoners of war of the Japanese. Five seamen, and four flyboys. They looked ruefully at one another and pondered what gruesome fate awaited them.

Chapter 19: Railway of Death

Colonel Ito appeared like a moderately reasonable man to Herb, Tank, Ollie, Virgil, and Dixon. At least he looked reasonable compared to many of the Japanese they had encountered. He certainly didn't strike them as a sadistic taskmaster who drove men to their deaths needlessly. When the new prisoners arrived they were exceedingly interested in what Camp Changi had in store for them. Their companions in the raft that survived the sinking of the *Edwards* had been separated from them and taken to another work camp, but the two flyers and the three sailors had been kept together. They were each glad for the others. The camp was virtually deserted when they arrived; there were only a few guards and the one hundred thirty-two of them that the Nips had picked up from the water or the skirmishes that decimated Allied ranks and resulted in a few Allied surrenders. To the Japanese there was no such thing as honorable surrender, and Japanese all across the Pacific theater were killing Allies who attempted it. That these POWs had not been summarily executed was simply a matter of logistics—the Nips needed fresh bodies to build their railroad. Prisoners were dying daily, and new coolies were necessary if the rail line was going to be finished. The prisoners were just slave labor to the Japanese; men who they spent a pittance to feed and keep in miserable huts. As was true in all POW camps, the commandant found ways to reroute Red Cross packages and food supplies, and make a considerable profit for his pockets by selling the items to the local black market. Things were scarce these days, and they fetched a high price from those who could afford them.

Ito stood up on a soapbox to elevate himself above the new slaves, and spoke in a straightforward manner in halting English: "You men sent here to finish glorious railway linking Bangkok with Rangoon. This task is highest priority. Officers and enlisted men will work together. Work well and live. One day war be over, Dai Nippon be victorious, and if you are good boys maybe you go home to your families. You will be shown to quarters and join work detail in morning."

The Americans, Canadians, Brits, and Aussies were shown their sleeping quarters—filthy, overcrowded huts crawling with lice and other vermin. They had nothing of their own, just the few clothes on their backs and whatever little they had stuffed into their pockets that the Japanese had not taken from them. They began to walk through the huts and try to find beds that were not obviously occupied. It meant separating somewhat from their comrades, but they didn't want to take over bunks from other soldiers just so they could stick together. They knew much conflict would result if they came in as the new boys and inserted themselves too forcefully into the camp pecking order without getting the lay of the land. It was getting later in the day anyway, and the other POWs would be returning from their work detail soon to give them some guidance on where they could lay their bodies at night.

Two hours later a long line of men came shuffling into camp. Tank had never seen anything like it. Many of the men were little more than walking skeletons. The body language of every soldier communicated defeat and despair. Many of the men had open sores, almost none of the men had much more than rags hanging from their emaciated bodies, and the fight was completely gone from their spirits. With dull eyes the work crew looked at the newcomers. There were no smiles of greeting from them, only a mechanical recognition that here were more poor souls who would join them in their living nightmare.

Herb began to ask who was in command of the prisoners, and one Aussie told him, "That would be Captain Sumner. He's over there in the top bunk near the corner." Herb and Tank moved to the area to make an introduction and try to get oriented to life in the POW camp.

"Captain Sumner?" Herb inquired, sticking out his hand. "My name is Herbert Johnson, late of the USS *Edwards*, navy destroyer." "And I'm Tank Hogan, bomber pilot. We wanted to see you and get acquainted, find out how we could help." Sumner gave them a searching look, and commented, "Well I'll be, more Yanks. Seems you chaps are popping up everywhere! I suppose that means the States are sending more and more men to help us out over here. Glad to meet you. Sorry it's in these conditions though." He gave them both a welcoming handshake. "You'll have to take the available bunks rather at random I'm afraid. Most of the chaps are rather set where they are. But don't worry. Men are always dying, so you'll be able to move if the bunk you have now doesn't suit you." Herb and Tank were taken aback by the nonchalant way Sumner talked about the death of his men. They were to learn the hard way how familiar with it they too would become, how black humor was one of the few coping mechanisms left to them to counteract the horrors they would witness and experience. Sumner continued, "By the way, in hut number four there are a few more of you Americans. I suppose you'll want to link up with them. They can fill you in on the details of our little paradise here in the jungle."

Excited and yet dismayed by the thought of other Americans being in the prison, Herb, Tank, and the other Americans found a bunk, claimed it, and went together to find hut number four. When they got there and began to ask around, a British officer pointed them to one side of the hut, where they discovered three Americans. Herb, Tank, Ollie, Virgil, and Fred Dixon introduced themselves, shaking hands all around. "Welcome to Camp Changi, fellas," one of the old-timers said. "My name is Kit Anderson, and this is

Hack Wilson and Tasker Meadows. We're Marines who ran into some bad luck and ended up being the guests of the Japs here at their deluxe hotel." Ollie broached the subject that all the newcomers had on their minds. "What's it really like here? Looks like the Nips have been pretty rough on y'all." Anderson retorted, "Well, we've only been here a couple of months, but as you can see from the condition of some who have been here longer, it's no picnic. The Japs take us out every day, work us like dogs, feed us worse than dogs, flog us if we stop working, bayonet whoever falls to the side, and seem to enjoy having slaves to abuse." Tank thought about John Collins' remarks at boot camp on the article he had read about abuse of Japanese grunts by their superiors. He mentioned it now to Kit. "Yeah, we've seen a lot of that too," Anderson responded. "Those higher in rank treat those lower in rank with complete disrespect and beat them if they have any excuse at all. Everyone in the lower echelons is just cannon fodder to those above them. The guards, especially the Korean guards, then take it out on us. It's the classic story of the browbeaten husband kicking the dog, who then bites the cat."

Kit's eyes narrowed as he said, "Seriously, surviving this place is going to be the hardest thing any of us have ever done. We've already lost two American buddies, and as I said before, we've only been here two months." "What happened?" asked Tasker. "Well, four Marines came here,"

Kit continued, "along with a Navy ensign and a boatload of men from England and Australia. Richards, the Navy man, didn't take kindly to being whipped with bamboo sticks, so he struck back. They had him dig his own grave and then they beheaded him in front of the whole outfit. Kind of a motivational speech without words, you might say, and it worked like magic. You don't see anyone hitting back when the Japs begin to beat the daylights out of someone. The other casualty was a Marine named Horn. He was a little guy like me, but he gave in to depression, and he didn't last six weeks. Just kind of stopped eating or caring, and simply faded away one night. It's as though he wanted to die and get it over with. Horn had been declining for some time, and there was nothing we could say or do to shake him out of it. I've seen it happen now with many of the men who have been here longer than we have. Some keep the fire burning inside, hoping, stirring the flame to stay alive, with thoughts of a return home, an escape from the madness. Others call it quits. They can't handle living anymore. Attitude may not be everything, but it's the most important thing, if you want to stay alive."

Wilson and Meadows nodded their assent to Anderson's narrative. Tasker said, "To me, this is the war within the war, the psychological war, and we just can't let the enemy win it. I for one intend to do everything I can do to survive and tell the world about the treatment we've received."

147

One of the few pleasures accorded to the prisoners was their ability to insult the Japanese guards without the guards being aware of it. Each guard had a nickname, usually a derogatory one, and the Allied soldiers learned to talk about their tormentors right under their noses without being caught. Tasker and Hack filled in the newbies and pointed out each guard. Bantam (or Rooster) was the short, hyperactive, strutting guard with the little man syndrome. He loved to preen about and administer strokes with his bamboo cudgel, trying to prove his manhood. Happy Face was always grinning and actually wasn't cruel to the POWs, for which they were thankful. Bucktooth, Horseface, and Betty were the ugliest guards, as judged by a panel set up by Captain Sumner. Sumner knew the value of diverting the men's attention from the killing work and brutality. Mocking their captors helped the men diffuse a bit of the rage and frustration inside. One guard they nicknamed Vulture because it seemed he was always around when one of them died, and he seemed to enjoy watching it happen. Someone decided to name seven of the guards after the seven dwarves in the story of Snow White. It wasn't hard to do. Bashful was at the bottom of the guard hierarchy and often incurred the wrath of the other guards. Doc was the one guard who actually seemed to care about the distress and disease they suffered. He offered more than the usual amount of water to those who were thirsty and provided some torn fabric so some with the worst open sores could wrap themselves to keep some of the grime away from the festering wounds. The prisoners promised that if they were ever rescued and had a chance to take vengeance on the Nips, they would show him mercy. None of the guards were picked from elite Japanese families, so their average intelligence was a bit thin, but one particular guard seemed out of it most of the time, trying to figure out the score; and one nodded off continuously through the long, sultry days. Apparently he stayed up half the night playing cards. Dopey and Sleepy were easy names to give these two. The hardest choice came when they wanted to name Grumpy. Far too many of the guards were surly brutes, and the name could have fit any of them, but in the end one particularly nasty-tempered guard was chosen, after he had given an unusually severe beating to a private Wells-Burnet of the Royal Navy. The unfortunate Brit died three days later. Many of the men went to sleep dreaming of the day they could pay Grumpy back.

Kit, Hack, and Tasker were already familiar with camp life and how to identify and try to avoid the guards, but it had proven a more difficult thing for Tasker than for the others. Though the abuse seemed random from their oppressors, the prisoners after a time began to notice some patterns, one of which was that the Japanese, on average smaller than the Allies, seemed to enjoy picking on the largest prisoners more often than not. Tasker, who came into camp weighing nearly two hundred pounds, was one of the not-so-lucky recipients of the attacks. It didn't help that he had a big mouth and struggled to keep it shut. He had enough self-control to keep from any egregious backtalk, but he muttered a lot, and it didn't take much for Grumpy or Rooster to cane him a bit or kick him while he was bending over to work. Kit prayed hard for Tasker, remembering what had happened to Ensign Richards shortly after their arrival at the camp. Kit had lost too many friends already, and he wanted to keep Hack and Tasker alive if at all possible. Fortunately (or unfortunately), Tasker began to lose weight on the meager diet and slowly became less formidable looking, so the guards picked on the larger men from the new shipment and left him alone after a time.

Tank, Herb, and the other new arrivals began to get the hang of the routine and it didn't take long to see why so many of the men had such hollow eyes. It was a struggle to find a reason to keep on going. Each man tried to fill his mind with thoughts of home and hope of return, but with each new grinding day the thoughts became more mocking, the hope less and less sure. Herb kept remembering part of Abraham Cowley's poem from "The Mistress…"

When thoughts of Love I entertain, I meet no words but "Never," and "In vain."

"Never," alas! that dreadful name which fuels the infernal flame:

"Never" my time to come must waste; "In vain" torments the present and the past.

"In vain, in vain," said I; "In vain, in vain!" twice did I sadly cry;

"In vain, in vain!" the fields and floods reply.

No more shall fields or floods do so; for I to shades more dark and silent go:

All this world's noise appears to me a dull, ill-acted comedy...

It was hard for Herb not to agree with Solomon of old, who decided that life was a vanity. Herb said as much one night after an especially taxing day. Several of the work crew had died from their various abuses and tropical diseases, and it was hard to find reasons to keep on living. But where Herb had helped Ollie and Virgil through their academic difficulties at Navy boot camp, here one of them turned into the teacher. Ollie noticed Herb's melancholy mood, and said, "Herb, there's no reason to lower your head. They can't take away your dignity if you don't let them, and you have to remember the training we had. Quit thinking so much about what's way up ahead of you and concentrate on winning each little battle every day. Despair and hopelessness are the two worst enemies, worse than the

Japanese, and you have to fight them tooth and nail to beat them. When I was a youngster I used to get down-in-the-mouth, and my momma made me say five things I was thankful for. Wouldn't hurt you to try it right now."

Slowly the words sank into Herb's mind, and he gave a rueful smile. "You're right, Ollie. Let's see. I'm thankful for a great mom and dad, for a wonderful girlfriend waiting for me to come home, for still having relatively good health, for uplifting poems, and lastly, for having real good friends who know how to cheer me up!" Ollie grinned like an Alabama possum, and the Americans promised they would try to encourage each other when one of them got gloomy. As time went on, there was much to be gloomy about.

Chapter 20: A Few Grains of Rice

It had now been four months since Tank, Herb, and their friends had arrived at Camp Changi. Their days were mind-numbingly repetitive. Up at first light, they were fed a meager gruel consisting of broth of doubtful origin, weevily rice and perhaps a few rotting vegetables. The calories weren't enough to keep a small girl healthy, and for adult men forced to labor under a hot tropical sun for many hours each day, it was a slow death sentence, a starvation ration.

The men had to cut, clear, and lift trees standing in the way of their progress. They had to wheelbarrow thousands of tons of dirt to level the track, breaking up rocks into tinier rocks and smashing chunks of coral into powder to make concrete. They had to rip up the black floor of the jungle after hacking away the roots of mahogany and kamagong trees. The work was backbreaking, and all done in the close heavy heat of the merciless, uncaring, unseeing orb above them. Some men collapsed with heat exhaustion, and every so often the Japs would splash a bit of water in their faces to revive them. They needed workers to finish the project. But there were times the guards got so impatient with those they saw as shirkers that they just killed them where they lay and pulled their bodies out to add to the human debris so common in this god-forsaken foreign land. To add to their troubles, tropical diseases like malaria, beriberi, dengue fever, hepatitis, and worm diseases were rampant in the malnourished, exhausted men. Mosquito vectors carried pathogens nobody could see or defend themselves against, and there were no medicines to treat them when they contracted the parasites that made their lives more miserable than they already were, if that were possible. The food was rotten, the water contaminated, the insects vicious and ubiquitous. It was a wonder any man survived for more than a few weeks.

But the weeks went on, many of the men did survive, and slowly the rail line took shape. Colonel Ito had just received word of a new order the prisoners nicknamed Speedo, that the line had to be completed more quickly, or heads would roll. Speedo was the word the Japanese used when they wanted the prisoners to hurry up. Rooster and Grumpy were the worst at trying to implement this policy. "Speedo, speedo!" they would yell as they pushed the slaves to make ever faster time. The rate of rail laid per day increased slightly, but the rate of deaths increased even faster. The British and Australian officers with the highest rank tried to talk to Ito about it, reasoning with him that it was counterproductive to try to get undernourished men to work faster, only to see them die in greater numbers. "You'll never get the line built without workers, and you're killing them in greater numbers with this insanity." Ito was in a quandary. His superiors wanted the rail line finished quickly, but he had very limited resources in manpower and in food rations. He opted to keep the Speedo rule in place but increase the calories fed to the POWs, if only by ten percent or so. He was fighting a losing battle in his calculus. Sick, emaciated men just couldn't keep up the pace.

Tank had come down with malaria, suffering shaking chills, fever, head and body aches, and nausea. The others tried to stay near him while he worked and help him keep up, and it was a wonder that Rooster didn't fall upon him for a beating or worse, but fortunately his was a rather mild case and in a couple of days the worst had passed. Tank had been fearful of being considered disposable. There was no quinine available to treat those who had the malarial sporozoan *Plasmodium* in their system. He just had to will himself back to health. He had already seen what could happen to men who got too weak. The Japanese, having no further use for them, simply bayoneted them until they moved no more, then dumped their bodies in shallow, unmarked graves. An Aussie who had beriberi had described how his legs felt watery, how every time the heart pumped blood through his veins there was a throbbing pain, how it was anguish to keep trying to work with his body falling apart. He couldn't keep up and had been killed just two days ago. The Speedo directive was accelerating the number of casualties. Herb remembered his thoughts from his opening months on the *Edwards*, how the vast chasm between the Japanese and

American cultures had created this worst kind of war; how the Japanese thought of their enemies as *kichiku*—devils—and the phrase from the Japanese army manual that said, "if you kill them [your enemies] there will be no repercussions." *It matters what you are taught*, he thought to himself. *When the enemy becomes something other than fully human in your eyes, you can easily become a monster.*

Tank, already at reduced weight, lost another fifteen pounds during his bout with malaria, and he found he was hungrier than he had ever been in his life. It had been bad before, this slow starvation, but now his body ached for nutrients with an indescribable longing. *Nobody at home will ever experience this, and it will be impossible to explain it to them.* Food was all he could think of. That night, back in the miserable hut, Tank had to make another trip—fast—to the *benjo*. His nausea had left him, but the diarrhea persisted. Taking care of business, Tank noticed a couple of grains of rice lying on the floor of the outdoor facility. Who knows how they got there, but Tank picked them up, tried to brush off the dirt, and put them in his mouth. *How far I've come from the panhandle of Texas! If Mom and Dad could see me now. I am so hungry a few grains of filthy rice look good to me. Will I ever get home again, ever enjoy one of Mom's apple pies again?* Tank fell to weeping uncontrollably. *What had happened to his dreams of glory?* They had become a living nightmare of the worst kind. He had dropped bombs on targets and inflicted damage and casualties, but now he was experiencing war up close instead of from twenty thousand feet. It sure looked different down here. He remembered telling others how he would do his best to make sure he didn't have to survive floating on the ocean, or deal closely with the Japanese. He was going to stay thousands of feet above the war. But his best-laid plans had not panned out. War was just too unpredictable, Tank was in a living nightmare of the worst kind, and there was nothing he could do about it.

Chapter 21: The Cruelties of Camp Changi

The realization that you are dying sometimes comes in a flash, but at other times it comes in mean little doses. All of the men were at the point of psychological breakdown. The Japanese, despite their Speedo order, oftentimes delighted in torturing the minds of the POWs in their power. One day Colonel Ito pulled up his soapbox and made an announcement: "We discover that some of you have been planning mutiny against us here at Camp Changi. This must be punished to send message that escape is futile and energy be directed to working harder on railway." Seemingly at random, the Japanese separated seven prisoners from the ranks, all of them Australians, and began to march them out the gate. An hour and a half crawled by, with the prisoners who remained behind intensely waiting for some word as to the fate of their comrades. Shots echoed through the camp, and the men had their answer.

Or so they thought. In another fifteen minutes the seven doomed men all marched back into camp and the real story unfolded. One of the men acted as spokesman. "The dirty Japs took us into the jungle, gave us picks and shovels and told us to dig a big pit, one large enough to handle all seven of our bodies. As you know there is no escape plan, and Ito was well aware there was no plan. We figured it was just a way to get rid of a few more mouths to feed. So we dug. I for one found I could only think of how hard it was to have to dig my own grave. Well, we finally got the hole dug and were told to kneel down with our backs to the guards. We could hear them being given the order to come behind a man and execute him on the signal. Colonel Ito gave that signal and rifles blasted. Anticipating death, each of us fell into the hole, only to discover that the rotten Nips had all fired blanks, and that we weren't dead at all. Colonel Ito told us that the whole thing was a big joke he had thought up earlier the day before to lighten the mood in camp. I'll tell you what, if we ever get out of this place and I get a rifle in my hands, there won't be blanks in it when I use it on them, and I'm praying Ito is still here so I can pull a little prank on *him*."

The entire camp was emotionally spent, and Kit realized that the Japanese were good at playing mind games. The quickest way to demoralize and deflate your captive enemy is to keep them guessing, keep them cowed, make them use up emotional energy so there is little left with which to fight or plan. Well he for one wasn't going to let the enemy get to him. He promised himself that he would dig down deep and resist the temptation to give up and succumb to the dehumanizing conditions.

It wasn't easy. A few days after the fake execution prank, the prisoners were marching home from a long day's work when the sergeant in charge had the men halt. They were thirsty, having had no water for several hours, and there was a spring near the road, making a gurgling sound as it came down one of the hills. The men understood that the sergeant had halted here on purpose, just to torture the men, who were not given permission to slake their parched lips. The guards lolled toward the water, splashing it on their faces, filling canteens, and drinking deeply while watching the prisoners with mocking eyes. The sight of the spring, the fresh, pure water, was unbearable. For five cruel minutes they stood there in the late afternoon sun, still hot. Finally they were ordered to march again, without being permitted to cool their thirsty bodies with the life-giving liquid. John Patterson, an Aussie from Sydney, couldn't stand it anymore, and rushed to put his head in the spring. The Japanese had been expecting something like this. Several guards moved to beat him with their bamboo sticks, and Patterson's brother Harold impulsively rushed to his rescue. His thanks for such bravery was a worse beating than John received. The POWs thought surely that both men would die together, but they were roughly shoved back into line and were still on their feet when the workers got back to camp.

The punishment for the Patterson brothers wasn't over. Ito had them confined in the sweat box, a pernicious contraption that wouldn't allow a man to stretch to full length or stand up. It was covered with metal to increase the temperature inside to a hundred thirty degrees or more. The brothers were still in the box when the men returned the next day. How they survived no one could understand. Perhaps each survived so that the other would survive. It had happened before. Their hut mates treated them as kindly as possible that evening when they were released. All Herb could think was that this "ill-acted comedy" was getting more deranged by the day.

It so happened that the next day Allied bombers hit the line they had been working on for the past couple of weeks. A few of the bombs were direct hits, obliterating their hard-earned progress. In one of those topsy-turvy psychological twists of war, the prisoners were angry with their compatriots for destroying their work. One Brit said, "Blimey, it will take us a month to fix all that back up. And they could have hit one of us with those bombs. Who do they think they are?" Tank had to laugh inside. It hadn't been too many months ago that he had been piloting one of the planes dropping those bombs. He had never considered that one of his allies wouldn't appreciate it. *What a strange thing war is!*

Chapter 22: Go Nippon

"Why are we being rousted out?"

"Who knows? Every time they assemble us I'm afraid it will be for the last time. The Allies are pushing hard on them and they're jumpy. I'm thinking they don't want any witnesses to what's been happening here, and you know where that leaves us."

As they lined up to find out, Colonel Ito came out of his hut, mounted his little soap box, and addressed the ragged assembly of skeletons before him. "The Imperial Army send down direct order: All fit men go Nippon."

Tank, Herb, Kit, and the others couldn't believe what they were hearing. There wasn't a "fit" man among them. They were all hollow-eyed wisps of their former selves, ravaged by malaria, dysentery, or who knows what other awful jungle diseases they had contracted, not to mention the meager diet they had been on for months. Most of the men barely had clothing to cover their scrawny bodies; some with only loincloths they called "Jap-happies." Only a small percentage of the men even had boots. Foot coverings had rotted off long ago. Most, if they had shoes at all, wore rough wooden clogs they had fashioned to protect their feet. Fit? None were close to being fit.

They had been enslaved to build the Railway of Death through the densely forested jungles of Thailand and Burma, beaten to a pulp by sadistic Japanese and Korean guards, weakened by starvation rations and the inevitable jungle diseases that felled healthy men—how much more these abused and malnourished men. Then too they had seen men die, witnessed men being bayoneted or beheaded by the guards. Shadows of what they had been a year ago, physically and psychologically, they were barely hanging on, and they knew hundreds that had simply given up and died rather than struggle any more. Tank had lost nearly forty pounds; Tasker over fifty pounds; Herb almost thirty; and Kit was small to begin with. He didn't have a lot to lose. Thankfully he was in such great shape when captured that he was still on his feet, but he too looked like *death warmed over,* as his mother had been fond of saying when anybody looked sickly.

The war had turned decisively in favor of the Allies, and the inevitability of defeat for Japan was looming large in their collective psyche. In Thailand there was the possibility the prisoners might experience early liberation, because they knew from their contraband radio that the Japanese were on the run. But then again they could also experience early death, because the Japanese surely didn't intend for this many witnesses to remain and testify to the brutality of the POW experience. The men had dealt with the Japanese long enough to realize that they were not above killing every last one of them and trying to bury the evidence. In Japan perhaps they would receive more food and better treatment so they could be of more use to the enemy cause; but in Japan they also could languish behind barbed wire for a long time, even after the war was over. What should they hope for there? The thought of dying in some Japanese prison was not palatable to them.

"I'm all for going", said Ollie. "Anyplace has got to be better than this place."

"I don't know," responded Virgil. "Better the devil you know than the devil you don't know."

"But how could it get worse?"

"You may be right on that score. But here at least we're still alive, and still together."

"Yeah, I guess so. But there's a chance it could be better, and I'm thinking I'd like to take that chance."

"It's not up to you, you fool. The Nips will decide who goes and who stays."

Regardless, the railway was finished, and Tokyo had need of thousands of "fit" men to come to their aid to alleviate the shortage of manpower in the mines and factories making Japanese war materiel. And they weren't wasting any time deciding who was really fit, either. It seemed the Japanese chose at random—and sometimes with malice—without worrying about what unit guys were a part of. There was no unit integrity when they were done, and the boys were aware that in some cases intimate, life-saving friendships were being disrupted. They even saw the Patterson brothers separated, and understood that one or both of them, cut off from the most important relationship they had in this miserable place, would simply shrivel up and die without the other. It was amazing how strong your will to live could be if you were living so someone else could live too. They had proven that in their ordeal in the sweat box.

The guards finally came to the line where Kit, Herb, Ollie, Virgil, Dixon, and Tank were standing. All of them were pushed roughly toward the group selected for the Tokyo run. Thankfully Hack and Tasker, the two other Marines, who Kit searched for with anxious eyes, were part of the selected group too, so at least his two best friends would be going. Kit was saddened by the loss of Walter Horn, who he had tried to encourage and motivate, but at least these two guys—the guys with whom he had most in common—were still with him. On the one hand it was amazing how much the human body and psyche could take without succumbing, but on the other each time the body or soul was hammered, it became a little weaker. How much more could they take?

The selection process all happened so quickly there was little time to evaluate how they felt about it. No matter. It was useless to resist. The smallest unwillingness to accept orders had at times been met with brutal beatings, or worse, depending on the mood of the guards. Best to just comply and hope all turned out right. Maybe a journey to Tokyo would be better than staying here. And at least they weren't separated from one another. *Remember, make no friends.* Right. Without friends, why struggle so hard to survive? Kit believed if he had no friends to share his misery he probably would give up like Walter Horn had done. Relationships were the stuff of life. Without them, survival for survival's sake wasn't that appealing.

Chapter 23: The Chosen Men

Nine hundred men had been selected by the Japanese to "go Nippon." The commander of these fit men was Captain Sumner, who was highly respected by his subordinates, and liked by every American. They were grateful he had been selected to oversee them. Sumner arranged the men into six *kumis,* of one-hundred-fifty men each, with each *kumi* led by a *kumicho*, in this case an Australian lieutenant.

The Japanese officer in charge of the Japan Party was Lieutenant Yamada, and again the American prisoners considered themselves lucky. Yamada was a fortunate choice in their minds, because although he was austere and grim-looking, at least he was humane, which was far more than they could say about most of the guards and officers at Camp Changi, including the sadistic Colonel Ito. Yamada had stood up for the prisoners a few times in arguments with the Colonel, and Ito had backed down from some of the harsher punishments; Yamada had even publicly whipped one of the Korean guards for assaulting a POW. One time Yamada had stretched the rules and allowed POW musicians to come into his hut to give a concert and share some sake with him. There wasn't another officer like him in the whole camp. He had been educated partly in the United States, at Stanford of all places. Perhaps this gave him an ability to have empathy for the prisoners. Who knew? All the men understood was that this could be a whole lot of trouble if the wrong guards and leaders were taking them to Japan. Yamada was a pleasant surprise.

The Japan Party was in for more pleasant surprises. All the guards who took them to their new temporary location to prepare for leaving Thailand were now treating them with far better care and far less cruelty than usual. They attributed this to Yamada's influence. Apparently Yamada wanted the prisoners in the best shape possible when they arrived in the mother country, and that made sense from the Japanese point of view. The Japs first began to increase their food allowances, which thrilled every prisoner no end. They all had heard of being fattened up for slaughter, but with full bellies even slaughter didn't sound too bad. They were plain tired of being slowly starved to death. In the three days before their departure, their rations were doubled. This was cause for great rejoicing.

The outfit was divided for shipping to the coast into two four-hundred-fifty-man trainloads. The Japan Party was issued new clothing and arranged in neat rows to hear the parting words of the commandant as they left Changi. They had to stifle snickers at the gist of the speech from Ito, which was essentially that "All you men will be honored to know you are going to a peaceful and happy land and will not be harmed. Japan is a clean, snow-washed country, a land of milk and honey. In our country it is a sin to eat and not work, so to keep you all from being sinners, we shall allow you to work."

"What an honor!" whispered Tank. "I can hardly wait to get to the land of milk and honey. It's a cryin' shame that this clean country didn't try to keep us cleaner during our little stay here at their wayside inn, and they could have shared more of their milk and honey with us too." The others could see the irony of it all. They had been abused, starved, and worked nearly to death, and now the Japanese wanted to tout how moral they were in allowing them to work to death in the mother country to atone for sins. *Cultural divide, indeed!*

As the men started out the gate, they noticed that many of the prisoners left behind were waving goodbye and wiping away tears. They had experienced many horrors together, and some of them were closer than to any men they had known in their civilian lives. But the chosen men were off, and the others would remain behind, and there was nothing any of them could do about it. They could only wonder what would happen to the ones they left behind. Maybe they would be killed, maybe taken to other camps. But there was no way for them to know, because the Party was out the gate, heading out to face a devil it did not know.

Chapter 24: Leaving the Horrors Behind

The chosen men marched to the railway yard at Kanchanaburi, some thinking of the friends they'd left behind, wondering if they'd ever see them again. Others continued to thank God that they had friends with them on this unknown journey. The walk to the railway was not far, but a large number of them were still so weak they weren't sure they could make it, and they dreaded the outcome if they stumbled or fell or couldn't go on. They had seen enough of the Japanese impatience with such things. Thankfully they had been given more food for several days, and that gave them added strength. Still, the "fittest" among them were not in very good shape, and again the Japanese had seemingly picked the fit men at random. A few of the fittest were running on fumes.

They finally reached the loading area and boarded the train and began to move off. As the miles passed they re-entered the world of civilized men, slowly beginning to think of the horrors they had experienced on the Railway of Death and at Camp Changi as something that occurred in another life. At least they hoped so. None of them could predict what would happen the next month, or for that matter, what would happen the next minute. Herb observed, "After so many months with life hanging by a thread, just the ordinary appurtenances of civilization, the cars and buildings, roads and farms, normal people doing normal things, it's a bit overwhelming." Ollie heard the remark and rolled his eyes a bit at Herb's oversized vocabulary. "You got a poem for everything Herb. What about this?" Herb thought about it for a bit, and said, "Well, Robert Browning said his sun set only to rise again. That surely is appropriate. And Seneca, the Roman philosopher, said every new beginning comes from some other beginning's end. Here's to hope that our new beginning is the end of our miseries."

Ollie responded, "I never heard of Seneca, or even Mr. Browning, but I sure hope yore right. They say misery loves company, but I say let's keep the company and do without the misery."

Every now and then they got a glimpse of the ocean, and as they gazed at the sea, fear and longing intermixed in their souls. *Would we ever see home again? Oh that we could just board a ship and keep sailing and return again to those we loved in a seemingly far-off land and time!* Looking at the bright sun and placid ocean, Herb as always thought again of an appropriate poem, this time without prompting from Ollie...

"Once more I hear the everlasting sea breathing beneath the mountain's fragrant breast, Come unto Me, come unto Me, and I will give you rest. We have destroyed the Temple and in three days He hath

171

rebuilt it—all things are made new: and hark what wild throats pour His praise beneath the boundless blue. "

"That's beautiful, Herb. Did you write it?" Tank wasn't a poet, but he could appreciate a well-turned verse. He had listened earlier to Herb and Ollie discussing their new experiences.

Herb was in a reflective mood. "No. Alfred Noyes— *Resurrection* is the title, but I can't remember the rest."

"Well," Kit said, "it's appropriate. We've been resurrected in a way. Hopefully our new lives will be better than they have been the last year. It's hard to imagine them being worse."

All the men were beyond grateful that the guards were kinder to them now. They stopped for water, and discovered another lost sign of sophistication and technology; a new well had been dug deep into the earth, and the water was free of wogs. They drank it until they were bloated. It had been many months since they had enjoyed something as simple as a glass of clear water. Funny how longing increases the joy in simple things; how thirst makes water the most wonderful thing ever, and hunger is "the best seasoning." A simple ham sandwich would not have been a luxury to any of them had they been back home, but here in the wilderness after months of privation, it would have tasted like angels' food.

They were housed for a time in a temporary set of barracks that had tile roofs, concrete floors, beds with mattresses surrounded by mosquito netting, and best of all, electricity and toilets. Outside there was a volleyball court and miniature golf course. They thought they were dreaming. It was April first, and several guys joked that this was the best April Fools' trick anyone had ever played on them. They were afraid to sleep, because they just knew they'd wake up back in Changi. Their senses were overloaded.

But their trip was real, and so were the luxuries. At one stop the guards allowed them to bathe under one of the water pumps used to fill the train engine, and after refreshing themselves they experienced a last luxury before boarding, a trip down a tree-lined avenue towards their ship where they saw beautiful girls in beautiful dresses out walking, and the POWs just stared wide-eyed at them. They had almost forgotten that beautiful girls still existed. Along the way the Australians began to sing their favorite song with gusto, *Waltzing Matilda*. Kit and Dixon smiled. They always thought that was a funny song, and it seemed so silly now. But everyone was far more light-hearted than before, even though there still was the unknown out in front of them.

They were puzzled when they were told at the dock that their ships were not ready, and they had to go back to camp. "This is one camp I don't mind going back to," said Virgil.

"It beats Camp Changi by a country mile." Kit added, "Well, I guess ours isn't the only army where 'hurry up and wait' is the official motto." And wait they did, for several days. Nobody cared, because their situation was drastically improved from life at the work camp; they gained some weight back and were able to get over their sicknesses, at least to some degree. Finally, after days of alternately getting ready to depart and then waiting, going back to camp and arriving to debark, and after increasing their numbers by adding two groups of prisoners from other camps, over twenty-two hundred British and Australian POWs were boarded on the *Rakuyo Maru* and the *Kachidoki Maru*. Oh, and of course eight Americans boarded too.

Much of the latest delays had been to load rubber onto the ships, rubber to help the Japanese war effort. As each man filed up the gangway onto his respective ship he was handed a thirty-pound piece of rubber that had a handle. Several puzzled men asked the guards what was up, and they said, "In case ship sink, this life preserver."

Kit said he couldn't believe it; he didn't think the thing would hold itself up, much less a drowning man. *It's just a way for them to load more rubber aboard.*

So far this devil had been much easier to face than the devil they knew back at Changi, but Kit wasn't convinced still that it might not end up being worse. *They had a long way to go to reach Japan, and then what?* Nobody could possibly know what awaited them. Kit didn't like not knowing, but all he could do was trust that the Lord would watch over them and give them strength to face whatever the future held. None of them knew it yet, but their wartime adventures were far from over.

Chapter 25: Packed Like Sardines

Tank, Dixon, Herb, Ollie, Virgil, Kit, Hack, and Tasker were herded along with eleven hundred other prisoners onto the *Rakuyo Maru*, each carrying their thirty-pound piece of rubber. *Kumi* by *kumi* prisoners shuffled up the gangway to the forward deck, herded by Korean guards with pointed bamboo sticks. They noticed three large holds, two of which were battened down with planks covered in canvas and lashed down. The third was open, an airless chasm nine feet deep. Crowded already among the hundreds of men in the relative freedom of the deck, Tank couldn't handle the growing desperation that acute claustrophobia brings with the thought of being helplessly smothered in a hole. *Whatever else happens, I just can't go in that hold with all these men; I can't.* Flashbacks of being tied in the gunny sack, the loss of control, the stifling, imprisoning constriction, the irrational but totally complete panic he experienced as a young boy came back to haunt him. Blood pressure up, beginning to hyperventilate, sweating even more profusely if that were possible on the crowded, hot deck, Tank pondered the thought of jumping overboard and being gunned down in the water. Anything was better than that hold...except that the fear of living through the strafing only to be eaten by sharks shook him enough to give him pause and keep him from bolting.

Although for most there was a much lower degree of claustrophobic panic, a lot of the men agreed with Tank. Despite it being obvious the Japanese intended for them to occupy the hold, not a single man made the slightest move in that direction. On the contrary, men began to move all about the ship, occupying the banned areas and seeking to get as far away from the hold as possible. Everyone had the same thought in mind, *if I absolutely have to go down that ladder, I want to be near the end of the procession. At least then I'll be able to see the sky a bit and be near the opening.* The men fought over coveted spots where they thought they might get away from the prying eyes of the Japanese or Koreans. In a ship ready for sea, they became their own sea of jostling humanity, survival instinct raised to new levels as each fought for himself and his own sanity against his compassion for his companions and their needs.

The ship was still not ready to leave, and the men were on the deck for hours, eventually growing extremely thirsty in the tropical sun. A few had canteens, and they shared what they had with their closest mates, but it was far too little, and the canteens were quickly dry. Apparently the guards had no access to drinking water for the prisoners, and most of the POWs doubted the guards would get it for them even if they could. Two enterprising Brits found some Japanese troops billeted near the forecastle where there was a fresh water spigot. Bribing them with the few coins or trinkets they had, they were permitted to fill their canteens. Word of this fountain of life spread like wildfire, and soon hundreds of prisoners converged on the faucet. It wasn't long before those Japanese had the oddest assortment of prizes: badges, coins, the flotsam and jetsam of the poor prisoners. But at least for a little while the POWs' thirst was slaked.

Finally in mid-afternoon the British officers came forward with the bad news: there would be no issuance of water or food until the men entered the hold. The Americans watched as the other prisoners, still soldiers despite the abuse they had experienced at the hands of the Japanese, men who were accustomed to taking orders without flinching, finally flinched. Nobody moved. Loud grumbles were heard by eleven hundred men at once. The Koreans didn't have to speak English to know what was going on. They began to poke and prod with their bayonets or sharp sticks, and still the men resisted moving. Before long some were being seriously injured. Tank had fought to be nearest the guards and farthest from the hold. He knew that he was most likely to get stabbed a bit this way, but anything was preferable to being at the back of that huge mass of humanity being squeezed into the further recesses of the hold. All Tank could think of was how much like an open grave it appeared. Once, twice, three times Tank was pricked, and he danced out of the way as much as he could, but he was not going to go unless he absolutely had to, unless they had to carry his unconscious body down there. Herb, Dixon, and Kit had maneuvered close to Tank, but were still several rows back, in the crush of the main body of men. They couldn't protect him or even try to reason with him.

Slowly the mass of men moved backward as the guards unleashed curses, beating and prodding them to get them to move. It was an incredibly tense moment, and more than one prisoner wondered if they all could attack the guards in a coordinated effort and take over the ship. A few voiced this thought, but cooler heads prevailed, and most realized it could only end in hundreds of dead Allied soldiers covering the deck of the ship. Blood flowed freely from many wounds, including Tank's. Inevitably the men had to descend into the darkness. But some, like Tank, couldn't stand the strain. It was unbearably hot and close there in the hold, and some men thrashed violently and began to fight their way, panic-stricken, back towards the ladder. Others passed out, and their mates tried in vain to pick them up and move them back against the descending hordes. Both British and Japanese officers realized that things were untenable, and they had a quick conference.

Lieutenant Yamada compromised and told the POWs that if their officers guaranteed no monkey business the sickest men in their ranks plus four hundred others could stay on deck, and the men on deck would be rotated with those in the hold so that each man had a few hours to breathe pure air. This would also limit the overcrowding in the hold to make it more tolerable. Close to seven hundred men went back down the ladder, fearful but in good order, and the sickest men on board got to stay on deck. Fortunately for Tank, he now had three gaping wounds on his body, so he qualified as sick enough to be permitted the relative freedom of the foredeck. The pain was constant and unmerciful, but at least he could hurt in open air. And as much as he hated sharks, he almost would have preferred swimming with them to being herded into that horrible, horrible hold.

As the ship slipped her moorings and headed out to sea, the minutes glided by, but they seemed like hours to Herb, Kit, and the others who had gone into the hold for the first watch. The fetid air was hot like a blast furnace, and they were instantly covered in sweat. The men were pressed in the hold, a profusion of sweaty, smelly bodies that caused near panic again among most of them. Some again passed out from the stress. Everyone's breathing was labored. It was like nothing any of them had ever experienced. Men desperately clung to the ladderway to keep from being pushed further into the maelstrom of bodies. The heat was insufferable and the stench horrible beyond description. Kit tried desperately to compartmentalize, to think of hunting bear or elk in the mountains, to remember every detail of those trips so he could get his mind off the living hell of being trapped in the hold. For blessed minutes at a time the strategy worked, but the reality of his situation would come rushing back upon him, and he had to fight with all his willpower to keep from panicking.

Finally it was time to rotate men onto the deck and from the deck into the hold. It was major chaos, but finally Kit and Herb could breathe again, and they searched for Tank. Despite the fact they were still prisoners, despite their hardships, and despite the unpleasant smells of the ship, just to breathe again, to be removed from the foul dungeon below, was the sweetest feeling Herb had ever known. *Einstein is famous for relativity,* Herb thought. *Well, this is another form of relativity. Relative to being down there, this is almost like heaven.*

Chapter 26: On the South China Sea

The *Rakuyo Maru* containing the Americans and her sister ship, *Kachidoki Maru,* were surrounded by a number of other craft into a box-like caravan for the journey to the Land of the Rising Sun. The destroyer *Shikinami* took the lead, and three destroyer escorts took up flank and stern positions. There were also two heavily-laden oil tankers in the middle of the convoy. They set a course for Formosa Strait and proceeded at about eleven knots, zigzagging every six to seven minutes to evade possible submarine attack. In addition to these precautions two escort planes buzzed overhead, searching the calm ocean for the dark shadow of a submarine at periscope depth. The American POWs were glad to see all the protection. Herb, the most knowledgeable seaman among them, said the U.S. Navy wouldn't attack them anyway because surely the Japanese had sent a message letting them know they carried Allied prisoners on some of the vessels. "It's the smartest thing the Japanese could do," he said, "It guarantees the safe passage of the whole convoy that way."

The sea was like glass, hardly a ripple upon the smooth Pacific, and Herb thought about *The Rime of Ancient Mariner* by Samuel Taylor Coleridge, how in the old sailing days the ship would have been *like a painted ship upon a painted ocean.* Everyone was glad they now lived in the days of powerful engines that needed no wind to take the huge vessels forward. To be stuck out here not moving, having to spend time in that ghastly hold, would have been purgatory indeed.

Tasker said, "The ocean is beautiful, I'll give it that. I've never thought much about getting out on the water, but as long as it's this calm it's not too bad. I hear the North Atlantic is a different story."

"You've got that right," Herb declaimed. "They don't call it the stormy Atlantic for nothing. You landlubbers would be petrified to ply those waters. I've been out on a small sailboat in thirty-knot winds and fourteen-foot waves, and my boat was only fifteen feet long. At least here the waters are calm and warm. In the deep Atlantic waves can be fifty to ninety feet high in the middle of a big storm. There you'd be dead from hypothermia anyway in a few minutes if you took a dunking. You wouldn't have to worry about drowning. I don't know if any of you read about the sinking of the British ship *City of Benares*. It was carrying ninety children ages five to fifteen to Canada to escape the German Luftwaffe's bombing of England in nineteen forty, but a U-boat sunk the ship and most of those children died of hypothermia. A few did survive and lived to tell the tale. But hey Tank, at least you wouldn't have to worry about sharks there. Here they are all around us, and the water is clear enough to see them coming in to make a meal of your legs."

"Pretty funny, Ensign Johnson. Don't I have enough trouble with my bleeding and pains without you reminding me things could even be worse?"

"Sorry, Tank, it's not my fault you crashed into the ocean and then we got hit by that kamikaze plane. Just stick by me if we ever get into the water. It's like a second home to me." Tank couldn't help but think *it's becoming like a second home to me, too.*

Fortunately for the men as the journey continued hour after hour the guards relaxed quite a bit, and slowly some of the men nearest the opening to the hold were able to sneak out on deck, lessening the crowding below. Eventually there were over a thousand men on deck at one time, but as long as they didn't cause trouble the Japanese and Koreans let them be. Oddly enough, some of the men seemed to prefer the hold to topside. The burning tropical sun wasn't their friend, and every possible shaded place was occupied, leaving most of the men under the full fury of the Asian sun.

At night it cooled perceptibly, but the oven of a hold merely went from "high heat" to "low heat." Instead of being fried the men felt like they were in a crock pot, slowly being cooked to death. As the hours dragged by the men again began to be ravished with thirst. Many of the men in the hold sat in a cramped position, moaning and hoping to die. A number of men near the back of the hold apparently weren't sick enough to stay on deck, but they had dysentery and were too weak to get out quickly, so the stench, if possible, became even worse, something out of a bizarre nightmare. Still, Herb had read Winston Churchill's assessment of war, that the human body can stand far more than we think, and to some degree the prisoners' noses became accommodated to the worst smells. If misery loves company, lots of utterly miserable men had lots of company.

Amazingly, in the terrible situation, to while away the time, some of the POWs in the hold felt some singing would help. The guards went wild and yelled at them to stop, but the guards, although not the brightest of Nippon's soldiery, weren't dumb enough to enter the swine-pit of the hold to bring order, so the Allies continued to belt out song after song. At least if it made the enemy angry it had the effect of cheering up the Allies, if only for a short time. For men as debased and abused as these men, any way to fight back brought them much pleasure.

The men were also getting ravenously hungry. "Fattened" up a bit before the trip, they still were nowhere near their normal weight; many had been progressively starved for many months. There was plenty of rice on ship, but the Japanese only allowed one Allied cook to use one large pot to boil it in, and he was trying to provide three meals a day for over a thousand men. It was an impossible task. Feeding times were chaotic and dangerous, with men trying to cut in line and a lot of bad language, shoving, and even fisticuffs. Some of the men were so hungry that it appeared they were eyeing their comrades to see who would be the tastiest if it came down to cannibalism.

But the worst was the need for water. Some of the rice was cooked in saltwater, adding to their desperate situation; and of course they were sweating much of their water out by the gallon in the oppressive heat. Dixon decided he'd had enough of the nonsense and with bravura bordering on the insane, boldly waltzed by two guards and slipped into a stateroom in the passenger section of the ship. When the stunned guards came after him he feigned being sick. "Bioki. Benjo—sick, toilet." Amazingly the guards allowed him to go into the empty bathroom, use it, and while there he filled his canteen with clean water.

When he returned all Kit could say was, "Well, if you ain't the cock of the walk. I thought they'd keelhaul you for sure for that stunt." Dixon shared the water with the other Americans, and it helped them, but they were still in a bad way. They had been on the ocean now for three days, and many of the POWs were declining. Four had already died, and the British officers had complained to Yamada, convincing him that it would be in his best interest to bring all the prisoners to Japan in the healthiest state possible so they could work. Yamada ordered the guards to bring more water to the men, and allowed the prisoners to wash themselves with the hoses attached to pumps that brought up saltwater to be used in case of fire. To get some of the thick grime, sweat, and excrement cleansed from their filthy bodies was a luxury that made a huge difference in everyone's perspective, and they were in for more good news within a few hours.

That night, blessing of blessings, a torrential rain poured from the skies. The POWs danced in it, mouths agape, relishing the delicious pure water washing their faces and bodies. They filled every canteen, mess tin, and anything else they could find that would hold water, and there were many shouts of thanks to the Lord for the unexpected bounty.

Tasker commented, "Here we are, surrounded by hundreds of thousands of square miles of water, but we go delirious when it rains."

Herb, again quoting Coleridge and the *Ancient Mariner*, simply said "Water, water, everywhere; nor any drop to drink." *What would it be like to be floating on that huge ocean with no water to drink,* thought Tank? *Death would be a far greater blessing if that were my fate.*

As they drew closer and closer to Japan, the guards became more and more nervous. There were lookouts posted everywhere it seemed, all with binoculars, scanning the horizon. Their fear of torpedo attack was palpable, and the prisoners could feel it in the air.

Herb once again was the voice of reason. "Remember, if we get hit, don't panic. Try to make sure your canteen is completely filled, get rid of your boots, and try to get something to cover your head. Don't throw a raft or flotation device on somebody already in the water, be sure the water is clear of men and objects before you jump, and jump ship opposite the side where the torpedo enters if you can or you might be sucked into the hole it creates. Obviously swim away from oil or flames and with the current if possible. And whatever else you do, don't abandon ship until you are sure it's sinking."

"Yeah," Tasker said. "It would be Tank's luck to jump prematurely and be the only one in the water when the sharks come for dinner."

Everyone laughed at the gag, even Tank, although it was a nervous laugh that disguised the real concrete fear he felt about going in the water again. Nightmares of the plane crash, the *Edwards* going down, and his two raft trips, with his shark tag-alongs, were still with him. *Surely the Japs radioed our friends to let them know not to shoot at us. Surely!*

Chapter 27: The Enemy Below

George Kilpatrick was not in a good mood. At thirty-two-years-old he was the youngest submarine captain in the U.S. fleet, new commander of the ship *Growler*, and he wanted to prove that he deserved the honor. Graduate of the Naval Academy, class of nineteen thirty-six, he had been frustrated so far in the war. As a junior officer on two different subs he had been on unlucky voyages that had come up empty. Each time his ship had gotten off some torpedoes, but inclement weather, lack of good targets, and sharp enemy lookouts had foiled them time and again. George had also been influenced by his captains' attitude toward the torpedoes, believing as they did that the missiles were defective even though the admirals continued to argue that they were fine and it was the sailors who were defective in their aim. Kilpatrick began to feel the same way as his sub commanders, and was more than irritated with the attitude of those in the Bureau of Ordnance. He knew that numerous reports were piling up there about the frustration of the commanders with their arms, and that, as of yet, the complaints had fallen on deaf ears. *How are we supposed to fight a war without good weaponry?* George had heard about the *Seawolf*, commanded by Frederick Warder. It had penetrated a harbor near Luzon, fired four Mark XIV torpedoes armed with new magnetic detonators, and there were no explosions. On his way out of the harbor Warder fired four more torpedoes, and none of them detonated either. Warder was understandably furious, feeling he had wasted precious ammunition and seriously endangered his men. Something was definitely wrong with his torpedoes, and somebody needed to get that something corrected! *Growler* had been fitted with new torpedoes, and the men in charge swore that they were better and the detonation problems had been fixed. George sure hoped so. Some sailors called the torpedoes "pickles", and George realized a lot of the Navy pickles had been sour ones.

A hot-blooded though highly qualified young man, Kilpatrick finally got a chance to skipper his own boat. *Growler* was three-hundred-eleven feet from stem to stern with a beam of twenty-seven feet and ten torpedo tubes, six forward and four aft. She could carry twenty-four torpedoes, lovingly called "tin fish" by the crew, and had a four-inch-caliber deck gun for attacking smaller ships on the surface. Powered by four diesel engines on the surface and a huge two-hundred-fifty-cell battery when submerged, with a maximum surface speed of twenty knots and a maximum submerged speed of eight knots for an hour, she could also stay submerged much longer if she went more slowly, and she could dive safely to about four hundred feet.

Kilpatrick loved the Navy, especially submarines. He was well aware of the fact that submarine forces suffered the highest casualties of any part of the service, and that dying of slow suffocation was the unspoken nightmare of everyone on board. He also knew that the majority of military men couldn't stand the awful claustrophobia created by the tiny spaces men had to routinely navigate, with smells of diesel fuel and sweating bodies crammed close together when the sub was submerged for any length of time. Submariners were a special breed alright, with a unique kind of courage. He felt he was designed to be a submarine commander, and he relished the opportunity to prove it to the world. Submarines specialized in sneak attacks, and he thrilled at the hunt.

So far his maiden voyage as commander of *Growler* had been beset by more of the same boredom and missed opportunities he had grown tired of from his previous voyages. It wasn't always easy to find prey in the millions of square miles of the largest ocean on earth. *Growler* had chased and fired two torpedoes at a Japanese troop ship when they were west of Bataan peninsula, but missed, and had to dive and take evasive action as the ship's escort attacked. They had survived twelve different depth charge explosions and come away with no damage, but Kilpatrick burned with a passion to return to port having successfully downed a ship or two. Two nights later he fired six of his loaded missiles at three different ships in a convoy, but had no luck there either. He was becoming desperate to show his crew he knew how to damage the enemy. He didn't know it at the time, but another chance was about to present itself, in spades.

Nearly five thousand miles away, at Pearl Harbor, officers were experiencing a normal day at FRUPAC (Fleet Radio Unit, Pacific). A handful of brilliant and resolute scientists had worked for years to crack the Japanese military security code. Their success meant that the U.S. Navy could monitor much of the strategy and tactics of the Pacific war and make plans to counteract enemy plans. FRUPAC knew that the Japanese had an important convoy of ships heading through the South China Sea toward the Formosa Strait, and they knew the approximate schedule of the vessels.

Submarines often traveled in radio silence to avoid detection, but when big news had to be shared, communication was re-opened. Each time a sub was on the surface making speed and charging the battery, it monitored Pearl Harbor broadcast frequencies. If FRUPAC had a message for a certain group of subs, it was broadcast in code on those frequencies over several nights, until the message was received. Thus Harry Pendergast, communications officer aboard *Growler*, got the exciting news that an important convoy of Japanese ships was headed toward the Strait, and subs in the area were to move with all possible speed to intercept and destroy as many enemy ships as possible. Kilpatrick was asleep when Pendergast knocked on his stateroom door, but jumped from his bunk quickly and became almost instantly alert as he read the dispatch. "They've also alerted *Sailfish* and *Sealion*," Pendergast told Kilpatrick. "Looks like we'll be hunting as a pack."

With a determined glimmer in his eye, Kilpatrick responded, "I don't care how we hunt, as long as we bag some game this time. I've had it with wasted opportunities. I'm not going home empty this trip. When we get the chance this time we're not going to miss."

Chapter 28: Hunting a Convoy

When *Growler* received the signal about the victims they were to attack Kilpatrick's crew was hunting the Japanese west of Luzon in the Philippines, with no success to date. George told the navigator to plot a course to reach one hundred fifteen degrees east longitude by eighteen degrees forty minutes north latitude, the agreed upon rendezvous point for the three subs tasked with attacking the convoy in the Formosa Strait. Kilpatrick ordered her to make all speed on the surface with two of the engines, while using the other two to re-charge the batteries in case a fast dive was needed. The sub used its surface-search radar and sonar in the conning tower to keep a sharp watch out for enemy shipping and any Japanese antisubmarine aircraft or patrols.

A few hours later first-class Seaman Reynolds reported that the batteries were fully charged. "Alright, men, let's make some speed. All engines full ahead." George calculated that if there were no delays they would be in the perfect place for the convoy ambush in plenty of time to intercept it, and he was out for blood. FRUPAC had warned that there would be greatly intensified antisubmarine measures by the Japanese along the convoy's route—radar-equipped aircraft, hunter-killer groups, Japanese subs—the Allies had begun to wreak havoc on Japanese shipping, and the Nipponese were ready to stop the carnage, but George was determined nevertheless. "The closer we get to our destination the sharper we have to be", he warned his men. "The enemy will want to throw a surprise party for us if they catch us napping."

Arriving in the area in late evening, *Growler* met *Sailfish* and *Sealion* and communicated via signal code. *Growler* would take the middle position, with *Sailfish* south on its right flank and *Sealion* north on its left. Everyone moved into position and prepared for the strike. The wait wasn't long. In a few hours, about 0300, the convoy showed up, right on FRUPAC's calculated schedule. *Sailfish* struck first, landing a torpedo amidships on an oil tanker, blowing a huge hole in the side and catching it on fire, which brightly lit up the ebony sky. The other enemy ships scattered, but *Growler* was ready and moved in.

Kilpatrick got into position and fired four torpedoes, striking a freighter twice and a tanker once. Each explosion sent a thrill through the entire crew. They were jubilant. Finally, some success, with three hits out of the four projectiles they launched, no less! Now that was some shooting, with two ships crippled and sinking! And *Growler* wasn't done. A sub-destroyer gave chase, and began to pick up speed directly for Kilpatrick's position. Most commanders would immediately dive and try to weather the inevitable barrage of depth charges the destroyer would deploy, but Kilpatrick's blood was up, and it wasn't in his nature to back down, so instead of submerging, he gave orders to clear the deck. *Growler* would attack on the surface. As they moved to obey orders his men exchanged worried glances, knowing that their vessel was far more vulnerable on the surface. With a maximum speed of twenty knots compared to the forty-knot top-speed of a destroyer, running away wouldn't work, and shells began to hit the water near *Growler* as it moved away from the destroyer. Kilpatrick was on the bridge manning the target-bearing transmitter (TBT), a special pair of binoculars mounted over a gyro compass. Kilpatrick could see the silhouette of the big ship as her prow bathed in the faded light of the moon, and when he had lined up the target he pressed a button which transmitted information about its bearing to a torpedo data computer (TDC) that generated all the information and the firing solution to two officers who relayed the information to the torpedoes, which automatically adjusted themselves to the proper firing angle. As the Japanese ship pulled to within twenty-eight hundred yards of *Growler*, the skipper ordered the release of two torpedoes at ten-second intervals from the stern tubes, right down the throat of the enemy ship. The Japanese saw the torpedoes making foam in the dark, but too late to take evasive action, and ran right into both of them, the hunter immediately becoming the prey as loud explosions were heard, sparks flew in all directions and a puff of black smoke shot skyward. *Growler's* crew gave three cheers for their captain, and Kilpatrick was filled with understandable pride at their battle success. He knew that a sub's success was measured in the amount of tonnage it damaged or sent to the bottom, and he wanted the name of his sub, and his own name, to be associated with a successful voyage.

Now they wouldn't come home empty-handed. They had met the enemy, engaged him, and paid him back for some of the frustrations they had experienced. *Growler* had used several torpedoes in earlier missed opportunities, and with the shooting tonight had ten left, but in this battle she had made good use of the ones she had fired, the men and commander acquitting themselves well. *Apparently those faulty detonators had been fixed after all! Tonight the pickles were poppin'!*

With no more targets of opportunity in sight for the moment, George gave the signal to dive. He figured it would be best to lay low for a few hours, let the crew enjoy a well-deserved rest. "Men, you were magnificent. Congratulations on your success. This will be one to talk about with your wives or girlfriends, and of course gives you some bragging rights back on the base when we get some shore leave. Again, super job! Get some rest now. We may need it come morning." Despite the elation George felt, he was sure the Japanese that had escaped the duck-shoot had radioed their positions and the attack to their headquarters, and that antisubmarine aircraft would be out at daylight searching for them.

He was right on that one. The aircraft were out in force the next day, and *Growler* had to dive twice to avoid getting blown out of the water. One plane dropped two bombs that *"rattled the windows"* of the sub as it descended. *Cutting it a bit close there*, thought Kilpatrick. Maybe it's time to think about heading home to collect some more armament and report. But surely there would be at least one more target to send his remaining tin fish toward. He had three kills already, wonderful success on his maiden voyage as skipper. Still, it was hard to satisfy a guy like George Kilpatrick. He wanted to make it four victims, which would qualify him for a medal, and he'd hang around just a bit more to see if any luckless quarry came his way before he turned for home. Maybe he was greedy, but George wanted to impose the maximum damage possible on those who had attacked his country, and earn some honors as he did so. *Just let them come*, thought George. *Let's see if we can't bag another vessel before we head home.*

Chapter 29: Sitting Ducks

The Americans aboard *Rakuyo Maru* were in a reflective mood this morning. They had already noticed the Japanese were more and more nervous as they moved along toward Dai Nippon, and a few of them understood enough of the language that they knew why. "This next stretch of water is crawling with Allied submarines, fellas", Tasker said. "A major convoy got hit here a short time ago, and several ships were sunk."

"But remember", said Herb, "they have alerted our guys that they are transporting prisoners to Japan with this convoy. Our guys are smart enough to keep away. They might try to sink the oil tankers, but they will leave the troop transports alone. Besides, we have destroyer escort and are well protected. My biggest worry is being separated once we reach Japan and occupy the work stations."

"Looks like the guards aren't sure at all that everything is okay," Tank said. "They are as nervous as a bunch of cats in a room full of rocking chairs."

"Where do you get all those colloquialisms?" Herb asked. "Cats in a room full of rocking chairs?"

"I'm not sure what a colloquialism is", responded Tank, "but if you must know, my Granny used that phrase a lot when I was growing up. That phrase is kin to a 'calf staring at a new gate.' It means somebody is nervous. We love animal sayings where I come from." Herb shrugged his shoulders, realizing that his extensive vocabulary had been extended once again by his Southern friends.

While this discussion was going on, *Growler* and *Sealion* were at periscope depth, five miles away at 0700 hours and ready to pounce. It was a beautiful, peaceful day in the Pacific, a beautiful day for a turkey shoot. The Japanese convoy was protected, but the two American sub commanders wanted to bag a bit more game before they headed back east to Hawaii. *Sailfish* was low on torpedoes, and had already left for the islands for leave and refitting. It had already been a successful voyage for *Growler* and *Sealion*, but they salivated at the chance to send a few more Jap ships to the bottom. They had not been notified by FRUPAC about the presence of Allied POWs in the convoy because the Japanese had inexplicably failed to notify the Allies about them. As Herb had explained to his friends, it would only make sense for the Japanese to alert the Allies, if only for their own protection. Unaccountably they had not done so. It made no sense. *But then, what about war made sense, really?*

The POWs didn't know about the presence of uninformed comrades in the subs stalking them, and continued to converse on the deck as they sailed north by northeast toward their final destination. The placid sea and relative calm situation they had at present lulled them into a false sense of ease.

"Think we'll ever get home again?" Kit wondered aloud, voicing the thoughts that were on all their minds.

"Well, the good Lord has rescued us time and again. Maybe He has a bigger purpose for us out ahead, and will help us once more." Virgil certainly had hopes that they'd survive to tell their adventures to their kids. It seemed he always had a positive spin to put on their situation.

Inside the two subs the skippers were making their final approaches and preparing for their first shots. Aboard *Growler*, Kilpatrick knew that whatever he did he needed to make the shots count since he didn't have an unlimited supply, and he wanted to leave several of his torpedoes for use in case he needed to fight back when the inevitable pursuit took place. According to their pre-arranged strategy, *Sealion* was to open the attack on the Jap destroyer nearest the subs because he had more torpedoes available, and then *Growler* was to try for the troop ships and oil tanker. The Americans mistakenly thought the troop ships were transporting only Japanese troops back to the home islands.

Sealion, as planned, released two torpedoes toward the destroyer, and they both hit the enemy vessel perfectly. There were two huge explosions, followed by several more. Apparently one of the missiles had ignited some of the ordnance inside the vessel. Aboard the *Rakuyo Maru* the Americans heard a loud bang, and a guard came running by. They asked what was going on and the guard said in his broken English, "Island catch on fire." As they scanned the horizon they noticed a huge flame a half mile away and heard another mammoth detonation, and they saw one of their escorts sinking, fast.

Hack deadpanned, "Somebody's pulled the bottom out of that island, because she's gone." But the Japanese guard didn't hear the remark; he had disappeared to man battle stations. At first Kit felt great elation, thinking *our friends are here to rescue us.* Then he realized with an ominous dread that since they were shooting at the convoy, his friends probably knew nothing of their presence on the ship, and they could be gunning for the *Rakuyo Maru* next.

The crew on the Japanese vessel rushed here and there, clearly panic-stricken. It all would have been great fun for the Americans to watch, except the captain had given the rule that in the case of enemy attack, all prisoners had to go into the hold. Now those fearful guards turned their panic on the prisoners who were topside, and began to push and prod their human cargo toward the opening. The POWs obviously were not inclined to go into that hellish place again, especially since their ship might be the next one hit. But acting like maniacs, with a will and with rifles and fixed bayonets threatening, the panicked guards got nearly everyone into the hold, where the Allies immediately tried to stifle their own panic. Thankfully for Tank he was still too ill to move, or at least the Japanese believed it, and so he wasn't ordered to vacate the deck. The hold was too small, the air too close, the fear of being torpedoed too real for most of the men to stay very calm as more and more of them were shoved into the confining space. A few had a fatalistic attitude, feeling like they were doomed anyway, so why fight it?

But the majority continued to have a strong will to live, and so some jostled for a spot closer to the stairway, knowing that if they were hit they would need to get out of that hold as fast as possible and try to get off the ship before it sunk. A scene of greater pandemonium would be hard to imagine.

Rakuyo Maru began a fast zigzagging course, and the men in the hold could feel it, as though the ship itself was a living thing in panic. And there was good reason to panic. George Kilpatrick, blissfully unaware of any Allied soldiers in harm's way, had just launched two torpedoes at *Rakuyo Maru*; one slammed into the bow and the other hit further aft ten seconds later in the engine room. Tank saw it all from his perch on the deck. He told the man next to him, "Hey buddy, get ready for a swim. We're like sitting ducks, and here come the bullets." He could see the white trails of the missiles clearly as they approached the Japanese vessel, and he prepared for their impact. It was severe but not cataclysmic for him. To Tank it felt like two dull thuds because he was so far aft. Not so for the men in the hold. To those pushed to the furthest extremity of the holding pen, it was ear-splitting and nerve-shattering.

The bow shot caused the ship to fall forward and dig in to the saltwater, and the downward acceleration was felt by everyone on board. An enormous cascade of water washed over the forward deck, and a good portion of it went down the hold where the majority of prisoners had been stuffed. Some thought the ship had immediately gone under, and hysteria was the instant result. Terrified, they thought the end had come, and they thrashed and struck out, trying to breathe and move toward the ladder to get out. The prisoners closest to the ladder had to hold on for dear life, with tons of water pouring over them, trying to wash them away, some receiving nasty cuts on their arms and legs as the turbulent water tossed them around and threw them against the steel ladder.

The first deluge had passed, and now POWs began running up the steps as fast as they could. A few had the presence of mind to turn and help others get out of the hold as quickly as possible, and it was a good thing. Survival instinct had created a maelstrom of flying fists and flailing feet, as the men tried a mad rush for the ladder and a way out of their dark dungeon away from the press of their comrades. Chaos reigned until one brave soul—Herb couldn't tell who—yelled in an extremely loud voice with an Australian accent, ringing with authority, "Okay blokes, easy now! Let's help each other and get out nice and civil like."

Amazingly, like a slap in the face, it woke most of the prisoners up, greater calm ensued, and men were actually able to exit the hold much quicker now that there was some order. Men assisted each other, and soon the hold was empty. The guards obviously were now too busy themselves to care what the prisoners did. The two torpedoes had instantly killed an undetermined number of Japanese, those in the engine room and the forward artillery crew. It was enough to galvanize the rest of the Japanese into hurried motion to save their skins.

Kit, Herb, Ollie, Virgil, Tasker, Hack, and Fred Dixon, once out of the hold, gathered together and went in search of Tank. They found him hobbling around looking for them. The scene on deck was mayhem. Many Japanese had abandoned their battle stations and lowered lifeboats quickly, fighting each other like demons to get in them before the ship went down. *Rakuyo Maru* was sinking fast. Most of the useable lifeboats had already been lowered and were full of Japanese. The POWs ran to the last two but were sternly rebuffed by enemy soldiers with bayonets, who were obviously planning on using the boats themselves. The Nips had no intention of allowing an Allied soldier on one of the lifeboats.

So the POWs did what they did best—they improvised. About seventy-five percent of the prisoners had on their lifejackets, and they began to look for things that would float to help everyone once they were in the water. A number of the prisoners had canteens full of water, and a few more had the presence of mind to fill their empty ones before they did anything else. Survival at sea very often depended on having enough drinking water, rather than sufficient food. They found a stack of life rafts lashed to the deck and began to throw them overboard, where some of the men had already gone. There was an understandable fear of being sucked under when the big ship went down, and men began to jump overboard and clamber onto the rafts. One Brit forgot to fold his arms over the kapok pocket on his chest, and when he hit the water the pocket flew up and hit him in the chin so hard it nearly knocked him unconscious. Other soldiers without lifejackets on hit the water and never resurfaced.

Then another problem presented itself. After his two tin fish had hit *Rakuyo* Maru, Kilpatrick had turned his remaining two usable torpedoes toward an oil tanker sailing near the transport. Again his aim was perfect, and the tanker blew in two, catching fire and spreading burning oil across the water, and *Sealion* had also hit a tanker that was burning and spreading fire across the water. The POW ship had drifted toward the conflagration, and now the men entering the water had to contend with the possibility of being roasted alive as well as being sucked into the depths. Neither idea appealed to them. Tank remembered the training of swimming under an oil fire back in boot camp. He also remembered saying that he had no intention of being torpedoed and dumped in the ocean. With a wry smirk he realized he was about to go in the drink for the third time. He sure hoped he didn't need to swim under any oil fire though. He knew he couldn't make it.

Meanwhile, on top of the sinking ship, fast-thinking POWs were tossing planks, tables and chairs from the dining room, wooden hatch covers, chicken coops, oil drums, pieces of bamboo, anything they could find that might help keep them afloat. Unfortunately, some of the falling objects imperiled the safety of those already in the water. Kit had the presence of mind to scrounge a bit for some safety equipment and food. The Americans were determined to stay together, and he knew they would be in need of supplies. He estimated the ship would remain afloat for another ten minutes or so.

Herb had saved a life-raft for the Americans to use, and when they were all assembled, he took command. The other men trusted his judgment, and listened as he gave instructions. The two best swimmers, Ollie and Virgil, jumped overboard and the others tossed out the raft so they could swim towards it when they entered the water. The two seamen successfully boarded and began to use the oars to position the raft to receive the others. Tank, injured because of the abuse he had received from the guards for refusing to go into the hold, was lowered by ropes into the craft. Hack and Tasker tossed supplies to Ollie and Virgil and jumped overboard, to be picked up by the seamen manning the oars. Dixon was wearing his life jacket, but had failed to secure it snuggly around his body. The jump was between thirty and forty feet, and his momentum was enough to rip the jacket from his torso. He disappeared and didn't come to the surface. The men in the raft were close enough to see what happened, and made for the spot where they'd seen him enter the water. Ollie even stripped himself of his jacket and plunged underneath the waves looking for him, but to no avail. Dixon was seen no more. It hit Tank hard. Every member of his tight-knit crew that had been with him on his bomber was now gone. He alone, like "Ishmael" of old in the story of Moby Dick, he alone had escaped to tell about his experiences. He thought yet again about how hard war was, how much it took away from a man. But he had more immediate concerns at the moment. His wounds were seeping blood and fluid, and he had not been able to completely fill his canteen as Herb had recommended. He tried to put aside thoughts of Fred. He'd try to understand and cope with the loss later.

By the time Kit and Herb jumped into the Pacific some of the oil had spread from the sinking tanker near the *Rakuyo*

Maru, and they found themselves covered with the black gooey stuff as they surfaced and were pulled into the raft. At least this oil wasn't afire, but it was extremely irritating and noxious.

"Man, this stuff is in my eyes, up my nose, in my ears, everywhere!" Kit kept his eyes shut as his friends tried to wipe some of the thick slime from his face. "I think I swallowed some too," moaned Kit, and he proved it moments later as he vomited over the side. "Thanks, guys, I appreciate the TLC." It was obvious that Kit was going to have trouble with this added difficulty. Herb was silent, but needed the same help from his comrades to clear his face so he could see and begin to get his bearings. He knew he would be a valuable asset to his friends because of his experience on the water.

The Americans were together, except for the loss of Dixon, and they were alive. Ollie and Virgil were at the oars and pulled them away from the troop ship as it sank. They could hear the cries of some of the British and Australian men still in the water, but the seven of them filled the raft, and they were afraid that adding others would seriously jeopardize all of their chances of survival, so they didn't respond. It was very hard to bear the sounds of distress from the desperate men, but they hoped that some of their other comrades could come to their aid.

Men were in all kinds of situations. Some were floating on the thick planks that made decent rafts. Three men could get up on top of one of them fairly well, and more than that could use them for flotation if they lowered themselves in the water. Some of the tables and deck chairs were being used to keep men's heads above water. It was a free-for-all as men struggled to survive and tried to find the best possible flotation devices to help them get above the surface. The funniest moment came when they saw an Aussie floating on one of the portable outhouses that had lined the deck. "I'm free! I may be floating alone on a benjo in the wide Pacific, but I'm free!"

The Americans laughed at the half-delirious soldier, slap-happy to not have abusive enemy guards picking on him. Tank wondered if the sharks would be so kind when they found him. The poor fellow might wish to see some Japanese again if those predators showed up. As the hundreds of men in the Pacific began to find some stability on their sundry craft, all of them thought the same thing.

Chapter 30: Revenge

The POWs tried to stay together. They figured their chance of getting picked up by friendly forces was much greater if they produced a larger target to see, especially if it was an airplane looking for them. Unfortunately, as all of them fully realized, nobody would know to look for them. The submarines that had sunk the destroyer, the tanker, and the *Rakuyo Maru* were Allies, but they would have no way of knowing they had inadvertently placed their comrades in danger. Many of the British and Australian soldiers had gotten into the oil, and it covered them as it had Kit and Herb, and many of their situations were far worse than the Americans. A number of unfortunates had drifted into the oil fire and were consumed in the flames. Their cries were unearthly and unnerving. *What a nightmare of a way to go,* thought Tank. *Sharks, drowning or fire? None of those are really great options.* Despite their best efforts, swirling ocean currents were separating the survivors into groups.

The mixture of emotions among different individuals and even within the same individual was great. Exhilarated to be free of Japanese oppression, they were at the same time in great fear of shark attack, drowning, dying slowly of thirst, or being strafed by a Japanese patrol that might happen upon them. They knew they were hardly in great shape, and there were multiple ways their situation could change for the worse. As it turned out, the Japanese who hadn't made it to lifeboats had a much closer threat to their lives than shark attack.

Some of the Japanese who had loaded up lifeboats early and pulled away were still around, looking for any of their comrades who needed help. At that point several significant things happened within a relatively short space of time. A few of the Allies were in worse shape than the others, either because they had swallowed and been covered with more of the oil, or because they were alone and separated from the others, or because they had no lifejacket on and were fearful of drowning. The Americans watched as several of the Japanese boats pulled near these soldiers in distress, and ignoring the entreaties of the men in the water, refused to help. Some of the Allied servicemen swam to the Japanese boats and the Nips beat them off with oars. They heard one Japanese officer shout, "Do not come boat. We no pick you up. You come closer we open fire." Several of the struggling men couldn't make it further, slipped under the waves and were not seen again. The British and Aussies on nearby rafts saw what happened, and it was the last straw for some of them. They had been abused, belittled, tortured, and starved by their brutal captors, and now they could strike back.

There were several Japanese who had ended up in the water and been separated from the others and the boats, and they were on rafts with the Allies. Tank and the others

212

watched with horror as their Aussie and British comrades pulled down these enemies into the center of their various crafts, enemies they had been at first trying to save, and held them down, slowly choking the life out of them and muffling their cries as the Japanese lifeboats looked for survivors. Hack saw one Jap trying to get on board a raft where several British soldiers had a perch. One of the men was trying to keep him away with a piece of wood, but his mate said, "Here, let him aboard. He can join us." As soon as the enemy soldier was pulled onto the raft, the man who had welcomed him aboard promptly choked the life out of him. He slid the dead Jap back into the water and said with satisfaction, "That's one less."

Another raft containing four Aussies drifted by two Japanese sailors floating on a spar. The Allied soldiers actually left their raft so they could drown the two. One Aussie, a good swimmer, was actually looking for lone Japanese to throttle. Kit saw him swim to at least three separate enemy soldiers clinging to different types of debris and kill them one by one. A few of the rafts containing mostly Allied soldiers had been rather kind to the one or two or three Japanese aboard their makeshift rafts, apparently hoping that when the Japanese rescued their friends they would be helped as well. Finally realizing that the Japanese in the better boats were not going to help them, and were still behaving as enemies, they dispatched their extra passengers without hesitation. Ollie witnessed several of these incidents, and though shocked, understood to a degree. "God weeps over a fallen sparrow, but these hard-hearted Japs are willin' to allow hundreds of men to die a slow, tortuous death. I can see why the Aussies are taking their revenge."

The lifeboats containing the best-situated Japanese finally left the area, and their now lifeless fellows were dumped into the water by the POWs, Japanese soldiers who paid a high price for the lack of humanity in their countrymen. *All's fair in love and war,* the old saying goes. It was a savage and cruel thing, was war.

Herb was troubled by the sight. *War is a sad, sad thing,* he thought. *The Lord said, 'Vengeance is Mine, I will repay', but men are apt to take things into their own hands. I'm glad we weren't stuck with having to make a decision on who lives and who dies. There's been enough hatred and killing in this war for me. This truly is the worst kind of war.*

The seven Americans were in a raft that kept them out of the water, and because of that they actually moved faster and eventually farther away from the others. It wasn't too many hours before they had trouble seeing most of the other prisoners spreading out over the sea. So now, after the horrors of capture, Camp Changi, and after the uncertainty of the trip to Japan, the American POWs found themselves fighting for their lives once again. How much could they take? It was a question that haunted them all, and a question that would be answered soon enough.

Chapter 31: The Thankful Game

As the Allies drifted with the current, they were grateful for a number of things. They had each other, hundreds of men of like mind and common philosophy of life; many of the men were close friends. Most of them were in fairly good physical shape despite the low body weight and diseases they had suffered. At least the Japanese had collected the most "fit" men, and treating them like human beings for a spell—with more food, clean water, physical recreation, and a least a modicum of kindness—helping them be in much better shape for the journey. Had they been removed from Camp Changi as they were and shipped immediately, their chances of survival at this point would be almost nil.

Now the biggest enemies they faced were the unmerciful sun, the oil that coated many of their bodies, and most drastically, the need for water. A decent portion of the men had canteens, but among so many it wasn't much, and it wasn't going to last very long. In addition so many of the canteens were of WWI issue and had cork tops rather than screw-top caps, so the clean water within was quickly contaminated with saltwater.

Besides the lack of water, a few of the men, delirious at being "free" after many months in their hellish prison, and being good swimmers, spent a foolish amount of energy frolicking about in the water like it was a day at the beach.

Despite being warned by their comrades not to waste their energy, they did so anyway, and some of them succumbed much quicker to the conditions because of their folly.

There were other enemies that stalked them as well, enemies they had learned about in their training for lifeboat survival; enemies that were invisible, but were very real. Fear, anxiety, hopelessness, fatigue, selfishness, anger, all of these enemies of the mind would help determine who would live—and who would die—in the next hours. They would soon discover that the sea and the sun could be enemies just as remorseless as the Japanese.

At first, despite their condition and the several perils stalking them, most of the men had high hopes for rescue. Some even began to sing "Rule Brittania." Much of this was false hope, for who of their Allied friends even knew they were floating on the water, and how would they find them anyway in this vast, trackless emptiness? But *hope springs eternal in the breast*, the saying goes, and various scenarios for rescue or making landfall on the coast of China were discussed by different groups of men. The seven Americans were in better shape than men in some of the other groups, with some water still to share between them and a few bits of food that Kit had salvaged before they jumped, but Herb and Kit were still suffering from the oil that had stuck to them, and Kit's bowels were doing a dance because of the noxious stuff that he had gulped. Petroleum products just weren't made for absorption into the human body.

The burning sun mercilessly shone on them, and none of them had hats or caps for protection. It wasn't long until their faces, already tanned, had nevertheless burned red. They tried thinking through how much water they could consume, and came to realize that it wasn't going to last them much more than a day at best, and that was if they strictly rationed it. As time went on that first long day, their lips began to crack and the salt water stung when it splashed in their faces. They were already weak from hunger, so they distributed a morsel to each person, but it wasn't nearly enough to satisfy.

His wounds hurting constantly, thirsty and ravenously hungry, Tank began to use a technique he had practiced on the panhandle plains. *I can just tune this out*, he thought, *not think or feel anything for hours. It's just like hoeing the garden or watering the fruit trees or taking care of the livestock. I'll go to a different place in my mind and listen to the white noise and think of nothing.* His mental gymnastics had helped his mind stay strong in the misery of Camp Changi, and it helped him again. The sounds of the men around him, the splash of the ocean against the raft, everything faded into the background as Tank for a time mentally removed himself from his predicament. His body was still there, and in a sense it suffered, but it was as though his mind wouldn't allow itself to contemplate the suffering or become anxious about it. Incredibly it wasn't very long before the gentle swaying of the raft in the waves rocked him to sleep.

The others were having a harder time putting their present situation out of their consciousness. Ollie and Virgil tried playing the game a million other hungry men had played since the beginning: the game of "What's for Dinner?" It was a game they had played many times over the last year at Changi, and they were proficient at it. Virgil went first, describing in great detail how his mother would cook chicken-fried steak, mashed potatoes, green beans, homemade rolls, and salad. And of course no chicken-fried steak dinner was complete without homemade gravy. Lastly his family would eat the cherry cobbler. His mother was famous for her cherry cobbler. Virgil spent more than twenty minutes describing the production of the meal, and by the time he was done several of the men could almost smell it. Now it was Ollie's turn, and he tried to outdo Virgil in his description of *his* mother's favorite—crock-pot roast cooked with carrots, onions, and potatoes. He added the dessert too, telling the men of *his* mother's homemade cherry or peach cobbler topped with whipped cream. The men's stomachs were as empty as ever, but at least for a time they could forget their miseries and dream of going home to enjoy meals like this again.

Herb even wanted to get into the act, although the oil that still coated parts of his head was nearly driving him to distraction. "I'm sure those Southern dishes are great guys, but have you ever had lobster, with a side helping of clam chowder or oyster stew? He told the men the details, including how he used to dive for the lobsters himself and bring them home so his mother could cook them, but it was very hard for a guy from Alabama and a guy from Oklahoma to think about eating a huge "crawdad". Ollie had eaten clam chowder before but hadn't liked it, and neither Southerner had any use for oyster *anything*. It just didn't seem fitting food to them.

Anyway, the discussion helped them all forget their troubles just a bit, and pass the time during the endless day. Night slowly came, and with it relief from the glaring sun that sucked the life out of them. They passed around canteens for a small water ration, realized that they only had a sip or two apiece for the next day, and decided to play the "Thankful" game. Each man had to think of something he was thankful for, and they would go through three rounds, so everyone had to think hard, because it was against the rules to voice a thanks previously given.

Kit said he would start, and that he was thankful to have met Tasker and Hack, now two of his very best friends. "It's crazy isn't it? There has to be a war like this—and experiences like we've had—to build the kind of closeness nobody at home will ever understand."

Tasker and Hack nodded, and all could relate. Herb's turn came, and despite the discomfort he was going through, told how thankful he was for what his parents had taught him, how they had challenged him to "go and make the world a better place." He hoped his effort in the war was doing its small part to do that.

Tank was thankful for his folks too, and thankful to be part of a large family. "I learned so much not only from my mom and dad, but from my older brother and even my younger siblings. I learned to listen to my elders and care for those younger than me. I definitely think it made me more responsible." Ollie also had a big family, although he was almost the youngest, the sixth of seven. "I'm thankful I had so many people who told me what to do. I guess it got me ready for the military." Everyone chuckled at this admission, and realized that it wasn't necessarily a bad thing to learn to take orders.

Hack said, "I think it's important in life to learn both, to take orders and to give them. It gives order to the world, helps a person know where the boundaries are. When I get home I aim to be the boss of my dentist office, and rule it with a firm hand!" Kit and Tasker, who knew Hack best, smiled at his bravado, and Kit added, "As long as you don't act like Colonel Ito. You'll have a rebellion on your hands then." Everyone on the raft could relate to that statement, and the next man in the circle—Tasker—said he was thankful they had been among the chosen men to go to Japan, even though they now were floating on the ocean in a tiny raft. "At least we aren't in the hands of the Japanese, and we are free to chart our course and determine our destiny. And I'm thankful I'm here with you guys."

Tasker's words brought a more somber mood to the group. They all realized that in fact there was little they could do to determine their destiny. The winds and currents were going to carry them wherever they chose, the sun was going to slowly beat the life out of them, and unless it rained they weren't going to make it for another seventy-two hours, because they would be dead of thirst.

The Thankful game progressed however, and it reminded Tank of the old hymn "Count Your Blessings" that he had sung in church many times. He mentioned it, and quoted one of the lines, which went "So, amid the conflict whether great or small, do not be discouraged, God is over all; count your many blessings, angels will attend, help and comfort give you to your journey's end."

Herb perked up and said, "Tank, I thought you said you weren't a poet? That's a beautiful thought, and we ought to remember it." Tank said about the only poetry he knew probably came from those old hymns, and he finished the Thankful Game by adding, "The last thing I'm thankful for is that, in the fourteen hours since we went into the sea, we haven't seen one shark!" *Everyone* could say amen to that!

Chapter 32: Death on the Water

It had now been nearly fifty hours since the sinking of the *Rakuyo Maru,* and the seven American servicemen were in trouble. They had drifted away from most of the other groups of survivors, but could still see isolated batches clinging to their floating homes, bobbing gracefully on the swells of the Pacific. Thankfully the weather had been calm, but the sun's rays were unmerciful. They had all experienced the oppressive heat of the jungle, but here there was no shade and no relief, and the sun's rays reflected off the water to magnify the torture. They had finished all their water rations, and each man, with cracked lips and swollen tongues, could think of nothing but the precious, life-giving liquid.

Tank had heard that thirst was the greatest torment, and he now was a firm believer. He had been starved, beaten, and jabbed, but nothing compared to the longing he now felt for water. It occupied his every thought, and he couldn't make the longing go away for an instant. He tried his old trick of going to a different place in his mind to escape the obsession, but he couldn't shake his body's need for fluid. Each cell in his body was slowly dehydrating, and his life was ebbing away.

At least Tank was still in his right mind. Both Kit and Herb, who had been coated with oil, had begun to hallucinate and lose themselves hours ago. Herb had been babbling poetry for a long time now, rising in great crescendos and falling off in sad whispers. Virgil, suffering but still able to think clearly, tried for a time to comfort him and bring him back to reality, but it was a losing proposition. Ollie had a hard time believing Herb could even talk because his own tongue was so swollen, but Herb kept on. He said, "Milton had it right. 'The sun with more effectual beams had cheered the face of the earth, and dried the wet from drooping plant...' Boys, the sun has certainly done its job, and we're all dried out..." When Virgil tried to calm him Herb spoke even louder, "And quoting Milton again, 'All is not lost, the unconquerable will, and study of revenge, immortal hate, and the courage never to submit or yield.' Courage, lads, hang in there. It won't be long until we reach the other side." Once, after he had calmed down and seemed to sleep for awhile, he awoke with a start and began to cry out for water. "I want water! I want water!" The others didn't want to feel angry toward Herb's ravings, but they were overcome by their own needs and troubles, and they began to mutter at him to stop, or maybe they would stop him. Ollie and Virgil tried to calm him, and then they threatened him. Ollie even slapped him once, hard. Startled, Herb lay back and quietly spoke about his parents, about Karen, about getting home to her to marry her and start a family, about sailing ships and becoming a captain. Herb had a terrific vocabulary, and it was evident he intended to use it all up if he could before he

225

went down. Eventually, after hours of chattering, Herb became still.

The other men, almost comatose themselves, were faintly aware that a hush had settled on their raft, and at least in their subconscious they were grateful. The sea was a flat calm, perfectly still, but the men were too far gone to notice it much. Each man slid into an apathetic torpor, but eventually a splash over the side followed by a wild yelling brought them out of it a bit. Tank shook his head to clear the cobwebs and noticed that Herb was gone. His muddled head took a moment to understand—Herb was paddling away from the raft, calling to the others to follow him to the island. "Lads I've had a nice drink of water and I'm going home! Come and join me!" Tank realized with a start that Herb had given way to the urge to drink seawater, and that his body, already in a dehydrated state, was now in shock and that truly Herb was a raving lunatic. Herb was so far gone that he had taken off his life vest so that he could swim faster. He wasn't more than fifty yards from the raft when he offered up a final cry of "Jump in, guys!" and disappeared under the surface. Ollie and Virgil both jumped into the water and swam toward the spot, hoping against hope that he would come back up, but Herb was gone. Their emotions completely raw, both men broke down and began to weep, hugging one another in the water as Tank and Hack used their hands to row the raft toward them. It took a supreme effort, but the

226

men in the water finally regained their spots in the raft, and a desperate gloom fell upon them all.

Finally Ollie spoke. "He was a good friend, Herb was. I never would have gotten out of boot camp without him. He was high class. Curse this war, but I guess I never would have met a fella like him without it. He and I would never run in the same kind of company normally. Harvard. I barely graduated high school. I'm gonna miss those poems of his. I didn't understand half of them, but they was mighty pretty words nonetheless." Virgil nodded a silent assent.

Hours passed, and the men fell back into their lethargic inertia. They were fading fast it seemed, and Herb's death was a poison to their hopes. Unexpectedly they began to dream of men from far away, shouting. Kit finally grasped that the voices were real, and he tried to shake everyone else awake. "Hack, Hack, there are men yelling somewhere. Can you see what is happening?" Kit's eyes were so swollen by the oil in them and on them that he could barely lift his lids. Hack elevated himself a bit and gazed off into the distance. "Kit, you won't believe it, but there is a submarine that is taking some of the Aussies off their rafts!"

It was true. The *Sealion* had arrived and was in the act of rescuing as many men as its crew could find. The shouting was the voices of the Canadians, Brits and Aussies who were crying out to be noticed. The Americans began to lend their own voices to the noise. Hack thought the *Sealion* was perhaps a mile or so off their starboard bow. He took off his shirt and began to wave it wildly, hoping that he would be noticed. He didn't think anyone could hear them yelling over the soldiers who were much closer to the boat. Tank, Tasker, Ollie, and Virgil all began to paddle furiously toward the rescue boat. The raft was cumbersome at best, they were weak from their ordeal, and it seemed as if a current was moving against them. All these obstacles combined to make it agonizingly slow progress, but they moved close enough so that all except Kit could see the sub and the rescue process taking place. They had progressed another two hundred yards, close enough to hear someone from the sub yelling to the men in the water. They couldn't make it out, but they certainly understood the gist of it, because the sailor closed the sub hatch and it began to sail away toward the sinking sun.

Of all the miseries and tribulations they had suffered, none was crueler than to be so close to rescue and have their hopes dashed in this way. Mentally, Tasker had been through more than he could take. "Well, that's it, guys. We're not going to be saved so we might as well drown. It's faster than dying of this wretched thirst." He leaned over the side of the raft, and like Herb, drank deeply of the salty water. Hack tried to stop him, but it was too late. Within the hour Tasker began ranting and raving like Herb had done, without the flowery language. He got more and more agitated, muttering to himself and sometimes shouting to unseen comrades, and it was all the others could do to hold him down. Finally he collapsed into inactivity, and the raft became quiet again.

It was completely dark by now, and the silence of the raft and its occupants was both eerie and dreadful. It was as though a dark hand was slowly closing over the men and their lives were escaping as a sigh. All the men were near the end, and they knew it. The life had finally been beaten out of them, and all that remained was to meet their Maker. Sometime in the night that is what happened to Tasker Meadows. The big man with the big mouth opened it no more.

The others discovered the loss of their companion the next morning. Hack seemed to have no fear of drowning or sharks or even thirst. He was the only man still stubbornly clinging to hope. "I just am not going to accept the fact that I'm going to die. I've got a dentist practice to go home to, and nothing is going to stop me from getting back." Kit admired his courage, and tried to think along the same vein, but the oil still caused agonies, and the thirst was beyond comprehension. He found he just couldn't gin up Hack's confidence that he would get out of this alive. Walter was gone, Herb was gone, and now Tasker was gone. The last loss was the hardest for him. He couldn't help but think wryly about how bad a start they had. Kit could feel Tasker's body reeling from the punches he gave him all the way back at boot camp. *How long ago had that been?* Kit wondered. *Seems like a lifetime ago.* Make no friends. Right. All of Tank's crew was gone. Only Ollie and Virgil remained of the seamen he had come to know. And now only Hack was left of the men who had become his dearest friends on earth, the Marines that shared a common bond that no civilian would ever experience. *I'm proud of you Hack. I don't think I'm going to make it, but I hope you do. Start that dental practice back home. Get married and have a houseful of kids. I'm rooting for you.*

Chapter 33: George Gets the Shock of His Life

George Kilpatrick was feeling good. He had sunk enemy ships, his crew had performed bravely and professionally, his submarine was intact and not being chased by Japanese ships or planes, and he could turn his thoughts toward a return to base. He still had several torpedoes left, just in case. It was a caution taught to every submarine commander: you never knew when you were going to be hunted yourself, and you sure wanted something to shoot back with if that were the case.

George felt so good that he remained in the vicinity of the stricken convoy for half a day. The other Japanese ships had fled for their lives, *Growler* had sunk two more ships for a total of five in three days, and everyone on the crew knew that they would be the talk of the submarine service for this memorable voyage. George could envision the awards ceremony as they pinned the medal on his chest. But he wanted to help out *Sealion* if necessary. If everything was calm in a few hours, they would turn toward Pearl and begin the long journey home.

Sealion had also had some success, but it still had enough armament to attack another convoy if one were to come within striking distance. Nothing presented itself to the two American submarine commanders, and by late afternoon

Growler was ready to depart. Kilpatrick had his signalman let the other sub know of her intention. This having been done he asked his navigator to plot a course for the Hawaiian Islands, then told the helmsman to head for American waters. Finally he told the crew to stand down and go to normal stations so that they could begin to get a well-deserved rest—after they ate, of course.

The next twenty-four hours were remarkably calm, especially considering the excitement and adrenaline-pumping action of the previous several days. They encountered no ships, either enemy or friendly, and everyone was laying plans for their shore leave. They had girlfriends or wives to visit, some had children to see, and all longed for some wide open spaces where they could get off this cramped submarine and stretch their legs for awhile. It was a happy, contented crew making its way through calm waters. For a few blessed hours at least they could pretend there was no war going on.

The reverie of George and crew was shattered when the radioman received an urgent cable from *Sealion*. Agitated, he rushed to Captain Kilpatrick with the message, and George read with growing horror the communication he held in his hand. *Sealion* had reported that there were *Allied* troops on the transports they had sunk, and she was now in the process of picking up survivors. There were enough survivors that other subs or ships in the area were urgently needed for rescue efforts. Hundreds of men were still in the water!

George had never felt so sick in his life. All of his joy at the success of his voyage evaporated as he realized he had sunk a ship transporting his comrades, killing who knows how many of them and throwing the rest to the mercy of the cruel sea! The proud thoughts he had harbored of walking into the base with everyone gazing at him because of his war exploits now turned sour, and he understood that now instead of admiring glances he would receive icy stares; he, the commander of the submarine that had killed its own soldiers!

It was almost more than he could bear. How could he have known? Had he let his rage for glory blind him to the possibility that friendly forces were in harm's way? He fretted and fumed for several minutes, then realized he had to spring into action to try and make amends as best he could. He got moving immediately, got on the intercom and told his crew that there had been a terrible mistake, and that they were reversing course to go back to the area where the transport had been sunk. Everyone aboard had the wind completely knocked out of them, their elation and excitement over arriving as heroes in Hawaii punctured by the news. Not only would their shore leaves have to wait, they would now be identified with the ship that killed its comrades. Talk about the fickle winds of war. With leaden hearts the crew turned *Growler* back west toward the killing fields, praying desperately that they would find survivors in time to save them.

Chapter 34: Atonement

Heartsick, mind racing, George told his sailors to get every ounce of speed the *Growler* had in her. As they began to enter waters that might be patrolled by enemy craft George considered just for a moment the dangers present if he stayed on the surface and drove the ship as fast as possible, but the alternative, the thought that many more men could die if he didn't get there in time, brushed away all caution, and he didn't flinch. Kilpatrick's executive officer, his XO, was Jeremiah Sutterman, and he was a superb young officer, much in Kilpatrick's own image. Wise beyond his years, aggressive but fair with the men, and most of all steady and resolute, he admired George, but he felt it was his duty to warn him of the possible dangers lurking in the water around them.

"Skipper, permission to speak," he said as he approached George, who was looking at charts of their proposed route.

"Granted," replied Kilpatrick. "Speak your mind freely, Jeremiah."

"I've talked to some of the other officers, and we want you to know we're with you, George, although I'm sure you've considered the likely presence of enemy ships and aircraft as we continue to sail west."

"Yes, Jeremiah, I have. I'm sure all of you have also considered what will happen if we don't get there in time.

Those men, if they are alive, have been on that water a long time now. Sun, sharks, lack of water, enemy ships; who knows how many dangers *they* have surrounding *them*! We've just got to do something about it if we possibly can." George allowed some of the tension to creep into his voice, and Jeremiah understood.

Sutterman smiled a bit and added, "We're with you, George, a hundred percent. We just felt like it was our obligation to point out what could happen. Look, we're all dispirited about the whole thing, just like you are; but regardless, we don't even know if any men are still left alive out there. We're taking an awful chance to plunge ahead this way. Like I told you, nobody is criticizing your decision. We all want to save those boys if we can."

George breathed out a huge sigh. "I appreciate your support, Jeremiah. I'll convey my thanks to the other officers later as well. But as I'm sure you are aware, I must take full responsibility for what happened out there, and maybe in some very small way I can make up for it by rescuing a few of those men. I know it's not much, but it's the least I can do...the least *we* can do."

"George, I know it doesn't help much, but there was no way for you to know who was on that transport. FRUPAC didn't know and the Japanese didn't tell anyone. Only God knew, and George, you're not God. Don't take on yourself more than is your due."

"Thanks, Jeremiah. Everything you said makes sense. Still, it doesn't help much. Tell the officers we'll meet in thirty minutes in the board room."

On their raft, the Americans were faced with one of the hardest tasks they'd ever had to do. Tasker, having imbibed saltwater, had died during the night, and now they had to lower his body into the drink. There were only five of them left that had been together at Camp Changi. Amazingly, three branches of the military were still represented. Tank was the only flyer left, but Kit and Hack were fellow Marines, and Ollie and Virgil were part of the navy. There never was any intra-service rivalry among them however. Their shared experiences under Japanese cruelty had bonded them together into an extraordinarily close-knit group. It was almost more than they could do to let their buddy go over the side. At least to this point in their harrowing and deadly journey they had not had to face sharks. The thought of those creatures devouring their friend's body was too difficult to contemplate. As it was none of them watched as his body slid down into the depths. They all preferred to remember the Tasker Meadows who was alive and talking…incessantly talking. Kit, almost blinded by the oil in his eyes, asked who wanted to say a few words as they gave up their comrade to the wide sea.

237

Tank said hoarsely, "I'll try to say a bit. I want to say that I admired Tasker for trying so hard to conquer himself. It's a difficult thing to change who you are, but he went from being a blowhard to becoming the kind of guy you'd like to have on your football team, the kind of guy you'd like to hang out with. He was first-class."

Kit nodded and added, "I can't believe I'm saying this, and Hack will back me up on it, but I've never had a truer friend. And to think the very first day I met him I almost broke his jaw." Tears welled up in the little mountaineer's eyes, and he couldn't go on.

Virgil piped in, "Sometimes we just don't have the words to use to tell what somebody means to us. I sure come to like Tasker a lot. He was a solid guy. And I feel about Herb the way Kit feels about Tasker. I wish he was here now so he could quote us a nice poem about being friends. I want to live so's I can go see his folks back home in Massachusetts and tell 'em how much he meant to me."

"I'm with you on that Virgil," said Ollie. "You and I can go together. Neither of us is too smart, so it might take the both of us just to find his house, or even to find Massachusetts for that matter."

Hack had remained silent all this time, but his cracked lips painfully eked out a smile as he said, "That's the spirit, Virgil and Ollie. We need to live, if only just to tell everyone back home what happened to us during the war. We can't give up like Tasker did. Our fight isn't over yet. Surely the Lord hasn't kept us all alive this long without something good coming out of it. It's a miracle we survived Changi, and a miracle we made it out alive of the *Rakuyo Maru*. It's a miracle we're still here, and I'm betting there is at least one more miracle coming our way."

Hack's optimism was hard to keep up. They all realized deep in their souls that if they weren't found within twenty-four hours or so, none of them would be alive. Tank, who had suffered malaria at Changi and also been wounded on the deck of the *Rakuyo Maru*, was nearing the end. Kit as well. The oil had caused such havoc with him that, tough as he was, his body just couldn't take much more abuse from the toxins. The sun and their thirst were ever-present dangers, and each soldier slipped into gloomy thoughts despite his bravado of a few minutes ago. Ollie began to resign himself to his own mortality, began to think of how his folks and friends back home would react to the news that he had died. Then he wondered if they would ever know what really happened to him. Perhaps he would be declared missing in action, and everyone in his hometown would never be able to get closure.

After another few hours, the Americans, lost in utter misery and fighting despair, were unaware that similar experiences were being played out on the floating debris occupied by their British and Australian counterparts as every group from the sunken transport drifted further from each other with each passing hour. Hundreds had died from exposure, drinking seawater, and drowning while trying to swim to an island or ship that just didn't exist. Many of them still had on life jackets and added a macabre pattern of death to the flotsam and jetsam scattered over the water. One Brit told his comrades just before he sank out of sight that he was off to milk the cow, since that was one of his chores. "Can't disappoint Mum," he said. "She's counting on the milk to make butter and tarts." Those that still clung to life were in terrible shape. Burned by sun and oil exposure, lips and tongues swollen to grotesque shapes, nearly all in trance-like mental states, they didn't have long to live unless they were found quickly. Some who were near the *Sealion* when it picked up one batch from the water the day before were now buoyed by the hope that they too would be rescued, while others, like Tasker, had found the nearness of rescue without its fulfillment the last straw, and in their despondency they drank seawater or just released themselves from lifejacket and raft, and sank out of sight to be seen no more. Most of their friends were too far gone to do much about it. They had reached the point where they thought, *if they've had enough, who am I to say 'stay and keep on hoping'?*

Though they didn't know it, there now was reason to hope. *Sealion* had picked up survivors, and they had notified other Allied ships to come search the calm waters, including *Growler*. George and his crew had now reached the spot of the turkey shoot on the convoy, and they had done some research on the currents in the area and done some heavy thinking about where survivors might be located. There was a weak current bearing off to the west/northwest in these waters, and the men had been floating for several days. *Sealion* had given coordinates for the spot where it had picked up survivors, so Kilpatrick and company had a good idea where to start their patrol. *Growler* began to cruise slower now, heading in the direction where they would most likely spot any rafts. It was a monumental task, a huge ocean to survey, but they prayed hard for eyes to see, and every available man was topside looking for anything that would show where floating men might be, and most of the searchers had binoculars.

The sea was completely calm, and with binoculars the visibility was thirty miles at least. All of a sudden able seaman Joe Tinsley adjusted his binoculars and shouted, "hey, debris and rafts on the water at ten o'clock!" Several men corroborated the sighting, and the officer of the deck notified those below to adjust course. It was if an electric current flowed through the men of the *Growler* at the sighting, but they were still a bit wary. There was a rumor they had heard that the Japanese often used rafts and debris as a way to lure submarines into an area so they could attack.

The debris field seemed empty, but there were some bodies on a raft floating in the middle of it, and cautiously *Growler* slowed and its men yelled to attract the attention of any survivors. "Ahoy, there! USS *Growler* here to take on Allied survivors!"

There was a small rustling movement from one of the bodies in the raft, and then a response in a British accent, "I say, what in the devil took you so long?!" Smiles broke out on the faces of the *Growler's* crew who were topside, and preparations were made to bring the men aboard. The rescue party was led by torpedo-man Ted Morrison. He was one of the best swimmers on board, and he gathered other good swimmers so they could make their way to the raft and attach a lifeline to pull it up to the sub. As they approached the raft, they saw six men, men who, except for the gravity of the situation, looked comical. They had very little clothing on, a few had Japanese caps on they had found, and some were almost black from the oil that coated their emaciated bodies. Their faces were swollen, and some, like Kit in the American raft, had closed, swollen eyes from the oil. One British officer remarked, "First you Yanks shoot us down, then you take your sweet time about coming to the rescue. You Yanks are always late to the show." There was little rancor in his voice, however. It was obvious to the men who were there to help that the men on the raft saw the whole thing as the miracle they had been praying for.

Once the six men were on *Growler*, George met with the British officer in charge. He discovered that although many men had died, the officer was certain there were many others out there waiting to be picked up. "I can't tell you how many, but we've seen and heard men afloat out there, and that was earlier this morning, so I'm sure there is more rescue work to be done."

Bolstered by this good news, George told his men to care for the British survivors and keep watching for other groups. The men were brought down the hatchway into the submarine, and work began immediately to remove the encrusted oil from the bodies of those who had been covered by it. They were in the worst shape. They were rubbed down with diesel oil to dissolve some of the thick goo, wiped down vigorously, and then the submariners used torpedo propellant alcohol, or "pink lady," which seemed to work well as a solvent, and was easier on their skin than rubbing alcohol. Gently the submarine "nurses" washed around the eyes and the rest of the faces of the former POWs with warm, soapy water. Like Kit, some of the men could barely lift their eyelids, and none could see well. The rough sailors aboard the sub were not used to seeing the horrors of war up this close. They lived in a relatively clean environment inside the sub, and several were overcome by the foul-smelling, swollen skeletons they had pulled from the sea. One sailor volunteered to go up top and watch for more survivors. He just couldn't handle the grim realities of war in the claustrophobic environs inside the vessel.

It wasn't long until they discovered another three rafts that had managed to stay relatively close to one another. Getting to the survivors was gruesome business though, as *Growler* navigated not only through a heavy debris field, but one covered with many of the soldiers who had died with their life vests still on. They were floating, most face down, but some face up, in the water. Several searchers had to look away from the carnage. It was too overwhelming to think of the huge loss of life, and the human bodies everywhere made a macabre scene out of some horror movie. Within the hour another thirty-two men had been swept from the merciless ocean. *Growler's* sawbones and his assistant were kept busy with the influx of new patients, but everyone on board was heartened by the fact that they had saved at least thirty-eight souls from certain death, and many of *Growler's* crew, at the direction of their medic, became good at giving some much needed tender loving care to the stricken ones who had lived through the ordeal. They cleared room in the aft torpedo bay, and set up their triage center there. Here they applied gauze, antibiotic cream, sulfa powders and ointments, started intravenous fluid and glucose lines, and administered morphine to those who needed it. There was precious little room here to maneuver, but they managed, and within an hour the afflicted soldiers were resting much more comfortably. There was great hope among the sailors that all would make it.

All of a sudden another raft was sighted, this one off to larboard and about ten miles in the distance. *Growler* adjusted course and eagerly made for it. As Morrison and his rescue crew neared this newest find, they found two nearly comatose bodies and three wildly excited soldiers. "Ahoy, there, mates," shouted Morrison. We're from the American sub *Growler*, and we are ready to pick you up." To Morrison's surprise, an American voice with a strong Southern accent responded, "Y'all better hurry up and take us aboard. Some of us are just about done in."

Once on board the sub, Morrison notified captain Kilpatrick of the American men they had found. George was beside himself when he found out that some of his fellow countrymen had been saved from the sea. "I thought all we were looking for were Brits and Aussies. How in the world did you guys get in this mess?"

Ollie, barely able to stand but elated to be on board the submarine, spoke for them all. "Skipper, it's a long story, and I mean a looooong story!"

Chapter 35: On the Way Home

Growler spent the rest of the day scouring the Pacific looking for more survivors, but none were to be found, and it was now getting dark. George, after conferring with his officers, decided to head for Saipan, the nearest territory held by the Allies, and he told his men to keep *Growler* traveling at maximum speed. He knew that these men were still on the brink of survival, and they needed all the medical attention they could get, attention the *Growler* staff couldn't give them. As if to validate this decision, two of the Australian soldiers passed away in the middle of the night. Their bodies had suffered too much for them to pull through. Of the Americans, both Kit and Tank were in extremely bad shape. The little Marine had suffered almost beyond his ability to cope because of the oil coating his body, and only his innate toughness had kept him from succumbing already. He, like Kit Carson of old, was a tough little fellow. But like Carson, whose body had also gone through so very many hardships as he helped conquer the West, there was a limit to what even the hardiest man could handle. The men of Growler worked hard to clean up Kit and the other allies who had been doused in the oil slick, and slowly but surely they were able to remove much of the toxic petroleum product from them. Kit had been carried to the rescue vessel in a semi-conscious state, hours before, and he still had not really regained his senses. Delirious, Kit kept having fitful dreams of trying to see his surroundings as he hiked the Montana mountains, only to be frustrated time and again by an inability to open his eyes. His dreams unearthed his biggest fear—never being able to hunt again.

Tank was in a desperate way as well. The injuries he had suffered compounded his dehydrated state, as well as the recurring internal problems from the case of malaria he had suffered while at Camp Changi. He could no longer speak, and looked half-dead, like he was ready to go to his reward at any moment, and was hoping he wouldn't have to continue to fight for life much longer. Thankfully he, like Kit, was made of stern stuff. With an IV inserted to help him rehydrate Tank began to come around, though he said he was still "Weak as a kitten," when the doc asked how he felt. The doctor also was able to find some quinine pills to help Tank fight off the malarial attacks. With his wounds cleaned, a morphine shot, and the merciless sun no longer sapping his strength, Tank finally was resting comfortably in deep sleep and passed the point of greatest concern. All those attending him now felt confident he would make it.

Ollie, Virgil, and Hack, although in serious condition, were in much better shape than Tank or Kit, and once they had some fluids inside them, began to perk up remarkably well. They tried to give a rousing cheer for the crew of the *Growler*, but what came out was a funny sort of squawking sound, like sick crows cawing at a coyote. The British and Aussie survivors who were responding well to their treatment all joined them as they tried it again, and this time a more appropriate cheer went up. With forty-one men to care for, the always cramped quarters of the submarine were becoming unmanageable. "Doc" Osborn told his aides to move the fittest men into some of the crew's quarters. At hearing that the "fittest" were being moved, more than one Aussie set up a howl. "Remember blokes when Ito told us the fittest were going to Japan? I'm not sure I want to be one of the fittest anymore!" Everyone laughed at the joke, but they wondered how their fate would have been different if they had remained at Camp Changi. Did the Japanese kill all their comrades to leave no witnesses to the barbarisms of the camp? And what of their companions who had perished in the downing of the *Rakuyo Maru*? War—and life—strange things. Sometimes you just never knew which road to take, what the outcome would be, even which road you would have preferred. But they were still alive, that was enough for now, and they were going home.

Eventually Tank began to come out of the morphine-induced sleep, and as he did so another drama unfolded. As Tank began to open his eyes and look around, he felt his old enemy, claustrophobia, kick him in the gut. He was hooked to an IV, laying on a cot in a room completely filled with sick men and attendants, with little space to maneuver, and his eyes widened in fear. He began to hyperventilate and thrash around, drawing the attention of Doc Osborn. "Hey, settle down, soldier, you're okay. We've got you taken care of."

Tank was sweating bullets and trying unsuccessfully to control his emotions. "Doc, I've got to get up and get out of here so I can breathe!"

Hack had noticed the uproar and moved over to help. "Doc, he's real bad about closed-in places. He just can't handle it."

Osborn responded with some irritation, "Well he's on a submarine, and there is no place except topside where he can get some space. I'm a good medic, but not a miracle worker. See what you can do with him."

Hack was joined by Virgil, and they did their best to calm their friend. "Tank, it's going to be alright. Take some deep breaths and close your eyes. We're right here and we're not going to let anything happen to you."

With eyes shut tight, the presence of his friends helped Tank begin to get control of himself. He began muttering, "It's going to be okay, settle down," again and again. Finally his heartbeat slowed and his breathing began to ease. Virgil said, "It's good to see you ain't lost none of yore fightin' spirit, brother." Tank, eyes still shut to keep out the sights of the close confinement, smiled and nodded.

Ollie was with Kit while this melodrama was playing out, and he was concerned. The little man was breathing irregularly, and though the oil had been scrupulously cleaned from his body, many of the petroleum toxins had been absorbed, and it was touch-and-go. Another three soldiers who were in a similar predicament had died within the past couple of hours, and others, like Kit, were fighting for their lives. The men who had never been soaked in the oil were doing much better. They, and the sailors aboard *Growler*, were surprised at how their bodies bounced back after so much suffering. Some began to complain about being ravenously hungry, but Captain Kilpatrick had given strict orders to feed the men slowly. Better to go steady and deliberate than to allow the men to gorge themselves. He had heard stories of more than one survivor eating too much too quickly and almost losing his life over it. Their bodies needed time to recover and resume normal food intake. So the former POWs were given soup and a bit of bread, and for now that would have to do. They were still moving at top speed toward Saipan and their ETA was now six hours away.

Tank had slipped away into sleep again, and Virgil and Hack joined Ollie beside Kit. He looked so small and still, almost like a child in bed. But he didn't look good. They were afraid his desperate fight to live might be futile. Virgil quietly said, "Hey, y'all, let's pray to the good Lord right now, and ask for Him to help Kit make it. I can't stand the thought that he could come this close to rescue and slip away from us now." The others, with sober memories of the losses they had already suffered, with thoughts of Tasker and Herb and Fred Dixon and their other friends who weren't going to be coming home, assented to Virgil's request, and he led them in solemn intercession. "Lord, we're comin' to Your throne of grace, and askin' that you spare Kit's life. He's a good man, Lord, and he's got a family to go home to. This war has brought on us a lot of killin', and we know You've got a lot to do, but You told us in the Book to ask, and expect, and You'd hear and answer. Thank You for helping these men find us on our raft, and thank You that Tank is doin' better. Now it's Kit's turn."

The three friends decided to alternate in keeping watch over their sick companion. They knew that for their own health they needed to eat and drink some more, but they wanted to do that as quickly as possible so they could also check in on Tank. They believed he had passed through the most critical stage, but if there was something they could do to help him, they wanted to do it.

Two hours later Tank awoke in much better spirits, and ready to eat. He tried to get up, but Doc Osborn told him to just stay put. They'd bring him some soup and bread. "Doc, I'm ready to eat a steak with some cream butter on a nice baked potato instead," Tank said. He had already heard about the captain's order, and knew his request wouldn't get

251

very far, but he just had to say it. Doc Osborn smiled and responded, "Soldier, I'm just glad to see you've quit thrashing around. Stay steady here and we'll get you something to make you feel better. It's not steak, but when you heal up you'll be able to eat the biggest steak you can find."

Hack, who was watching Kit, grinned like a possum when his small Marine friend opened his eyes, albeit stiffly, and asked, "Hey, can a guy get some food around here?" Hack stifled his emotions, and said, "Well, we can't go around wasting grub on the little squirts. All of us big men gotta save back something for themselves." Kit smiled back and said weakly, "Friend, I don't want to have to take you to the woodshed like I did Meadows, but if you insist…" He found himself touching the hull of the sub, still wondering if all this was real, and he wasn't in a raft about to die. The cool steel was a comfort to him, a link to his new and welcome reality.

George had been in and out, checking on the progress of the survivors. He was saddened by the loss of the five men who had gone past the point of no return, but heartened by the thirty-eight who now seemed to be on the way to full recovery. Ollie and Virgil happened to be near him, and both noticed the sadness and regret in his eyes. Ollie ventured to speak to the grieving man.

"Captain, I'm Ollie Hill from Alabama, and I want you to know something."

"What is it?" Captain Kilpatrick asked.

"I can see that yore thinkin' yore to blame for all of the men who didn't make it. I understand how you could think that a way, but you done what you were ordered to do back there by shooting down the *Rakuyo Maru*, and you done what you were supposed to do by comin' back here to save us from the sea. You're a good man, Captain, and all of us on board owe our lives to you. Don't ever forget that. A man in yore situation can do a whole lot of dark broodin', and spend the rest of his life in regret, but that won't change what happened out there, and it won't help you or anybody else to torture yourself about it. You did the best you could to make up for it, and there's a lot of families that will get their sons back because you did. The Lord forgave those that nailed him to the cross, because He said they was ignorant of what they was doin'. He done forgive all of us for our sins that caused Him to have to hang there. He forgives you too, Captain. Let that be enough, and git on with yore life. And again, thank ya for savin' us."

George silently nodded, muttered something, and walked away. On the one hand what he had heard wasn't going to be enough to keep him from brooding. Regardless of the fact that he hadn't known he was shooting at his own men, his orders had resulted in hundreds of lost lives, hundreds of grieving families. But more than anything that had been said to him since that awful day he heard about the disaster, Ollie's warm and wise words began to heal some of the hurt. They, all of them, were on their way home. And home would be a place of rest for all of them, a place to forget—if they could—the horrors of the war.

Chapter 36: Recovery

The USS *Enterprise* made its way across the waters, carrying with it over a thousand injured troops and former POWs. They were going home. Over two years ago Army Chief of Staff George Marshall had recognized that in preparing for victory over its enemies the high command also needed to plan for the return or redeployment of tens of thousands of its soldiers. After D-Day the thought was that the war in Europe would be over by Christmas. This didn't happen, but by then getting ready to bring troops home had become a major operation for the U.S. military. Hence, *Operation Magic Carpet* was instituted, but it wasn't an operation of the U.S. Navy. They had their hands full preparing for the invasion of Japan, so the task fell to the Army, Coast Guard, and Merchant Marine branches. It was an enormous operation, and would grow into the largest effort to mass-transit human beings in the history of the world.

One question was 'how'? If troop transports, aircraft carriers, and destroyers were being used to carry the fight to the Japanese, what craft were left to bring home those boys who were coming home? And that brought up the second set of questions. *Who* was going home…and *when*? Italy had been conquered months ago. Now Germany had recently capitulated. Japan wasn't defeated yet, but they were on the run for sure, and there was a huge public outcry to bring boys home. Added to that was the Pentagon's realization that millions of soldiers without an enemy to fight were going to be a huge discipline problem, and a drain on already strained military budgets. Homesick G.I.'s, who had been training and fighting for upwards of three years, were clamoring for demobilization and repatriation…and right away.

The men who had been severely wounded or had been POWs were near the top of the list of those going back. When the European war ended there were three million U.S. troops to be dealt with there, and even though the fight continued in the Pacific, tens of thousands of those men were also ready to see their families. The *Enterprise* was an aircraft carrier, but now it functioned as a huge ferry to bring military personnel eastward from Hawaii to the California coast. Tank, Kit, Ollie, Virgil, and Hack enjoyed the trip immensely. There were movies on the hangar decks, fresh food, hot meals, sports, swimming, and ice cream to make the voyage pleasurable. Tank didn't swim much. Every time he went in the water he could feel those shark fins running up under his raft. He knew it was a silly thing, but old fears don't die easily. At least he had been able to suppress his claustrophobia enough to get off the submarine without totally losing his mind. Captain Kilpatrick had allowed him time topside with lookouts, and there the fresh air, abundant space, and freedom from restraint were tonics indeed.

Kit had been fitted with a patch over his left eye, the one most damaged by the dirt and oil he picked up after the *Rakuyo* sinking. His right eye was doing much better, and he believed it would heal up to be good as new. He was a bit worried about the left one, though. Without two good eyes it would be nearly impossible to hunt well. He needed them both for depth perception. He had spent some time on the hospital ship USS *Benevolence*, and the doctors had been magnificent in trying to restore his vision, but they could only do what they could do. *Oh well, leave it in the Lord's hands. At least I'm coming home in one piece. If all I ever have is one good eye I'll have to make do with that.*

Hack kept talking about opening his dentist's office, and Virgil and Ollie couldn't wait to get home to eat some of mom's special meals. They often talked about how they had whiled away the time on their raft, talking in detail about chicken fried steak, roast beef, potatoes, and cobbler. Now they would get to experience those dishes for real. Each mile closer to home made them smile a bit more.

One of the biggest pleasures they had on board was the presence of over a hundred war brides. Many of their wounded comrades had met these women in hospitals while recuperating, and some had wed and were bringing their women home to meet their families. The atmosphere on board was joyous and expectant, and the nightmares they had all experienced began to abate the further from the field of battle they traveled. Having women aboard helped them anticipate some normalcy once they arrived home. Maybe there was a girl out there for them somewhere. Maybe they could settle down and begin a family. They thought again of Herb, who had so hoped to return home to Karen. "I guess it just wasn't meant to be," said Ollie sadly.

Recovering of wounds meant a lot of things to a lot of people. For some it was the physical healing that had been promoted by good medical care, freedom from danger, good meals, pure water, and the thought that the war for them was ended. For others the psychological and emotional healing was even more significant. To see smiling faces instead of "the look" you saw in combat. To experience laughter and hope. To be able to plan for the future again, to think of marriage and children and careers. These thoughts were a balm to wounded souls, antibiotics to the canker of bitterness and despair that so many of the men had gone through. Especially for those who had been prisoners of war at Camp Changi and a dozen other places, the trip home was a much needed transition from the death, destruction, and decay of the Asian jungles.

For Tank, Kit, and the others, it was soul salve indeed. Here they could decompress, talk about their woes and their dreams, spend time with people they would soon leave but could never forget. They played the "Thankful Game" several times on that homeward voyage, remembering when they had played it on a tiny raft in the middle of the biggest ocean on earth, praying for a miraculous rescue. The rescue had happened, not soon enough for Tasker and Herb, but just in the nick of time for them. Tank pondered a bit about survivors' guilt. He didn't really feel guilty, exactly, but he did wonder why he had lived and others had not. Herb had such a great future in store, but he was gone. Fred Dixon was his last link to his flight crew. He hadn't ever come up after jumping off the *Rakuyo Maru*. Tasker had given up in despair. *The fortunes of war, how random they seemed to be.* He didn't really understand it all, but he promised himself that if God had kept him alive for some greater purpose, he would discover it and apply himself to fulfilling it. It was the least he could do.

Chapter 37: Someone Understands

Rear Admiral Jeffrey Jordan welcomed Captain Kilpatrick into his office. The bright morning Hawaiian sunshine promised another beautiful day on the island, but George was still in a gloomy mood, dreading this meeting. The war was in its final weeks, though nobody knew it for sure at the time. Plans were being developed for the final push through to the Japanese mainland, and desperate fighting still lay ahead. Germany had surrendered, and the war in Europe was over. Millions of soldiers were heading back to the States, apprehensive that they would have to remain in the military and go west to aid their comrades who had been in the Pacific theater. Many of them thought, *surely I haven't survived Hitler only to die on some forsaken island. Why can't the Japanese just give it up?*

But the Japanese weren't giving up, and, if possible, were fighting harder as the Allies got closer to Dai Nippon. There still was much struggle left in the die-hards, and like men of all time, they fought even more savagely as they neared their own homes.

George sat down in the plush chair and uncomfortably shifted his weight forward. Ever since the *Rakuyo Maru* disaster he had been pondering his official response with his superiors. Should he resign his commission? Ask for a transfer? Still struggling with his emotions, he just couldn't decide. Maybe Jordan and the rest of the brass had already decided for him. Anyway, it was time to face the music. Admiral Jordan began. "George, do you know how Stonewall Jackson died?" The question seemed out of place considering the situation, but George thought about it, and began to see a connection. "Yes sir. He was killed by friendly fire from his own troops. In many ways it was the turning point in the Civil War."

Jordan continued, "Yes, you might say that it was the turning point. George, since the invention of warfare men have accidentally killed their comrades. Fratricide is as old as war itself. And there is nothing we can do about it. Try as we might it's just a fact that people make mistakes. They see a target and shoot, because they are commanded to shoot, and in the heat of battle there often isn't time to make sure what you are shooting at. The problem has become worse as we've invented guns that shoot farther and farther. We often can't even see what we're shooting at. The boys in the Italian mountains were shooting at Germans who were miles away on distant hilltops. At least they hoped they were shooting at Germans and the shells weren't falling on their comrades. George, do you understand the point I'm trying to make?"

George was beginning to see the gist of the discussion. "I suppose, sir, that you are trying to let me know that what happened out there wasn't my fault, and that it not only could have happened to anyone but has happened to many others during the long history of warfare. I appreciate that, sir, but I..."

Jordan butted in with some intensity, "There are no buts here, George. Your task as a submarine commander was to harass the enemy to the maximum extent possible, to sink or damage his ships, to throw a monkey wrench in his supply lines, to prevent him from transporting troops to critical fighting arenas. You and your crew did that magnificently. FRUPAC ordered you to attack convoys in the South China Sea, and you did just that. They didn't know the *Rakuyo* was carrying our friends, and the Japanese didn't alert us to that fact. George, you were following orders, and doing a wonderful job of it. Don't you understand that you are not alone in this? The Japanese and FRUPAC are equally to blame. Others have shot their friends by accident, and had to deal with the guilt and the mental strain. Don't let this accident ruin the voyage or your career. You are no more responsible for what happened than I am, or the intelligence officers who gave you the information, or the man who actually pushed the button to release those torpedoes. We need more men like you, not less."

George let this sink in. "I have been in a quandary about what to do, sir. I want to do the right thing, the noble thing. It's been very hard to come to grips with it, actually."

Jordan repeated, "We need *more* men like you, George, not less. You have a conscience, and that's a great thing, but one of the reasons you make such a fine submarine commander is that you are aggressive, a hard charger. Men don't win wars with commanders who are timid. We need you back out on the water, George, and your men need you. Don't you think they feel badly as you do? They were just following orders, same as you. They were responsible for pulling the trigger, same as you. They need to see you let this go and take the fight to the enemy again. You can help them deal with this, George, by watching you deal with it in the right way. It's time to quit beating yourself up over it, and fight again."

George was thinking hard. Everyone had done their best to help him release the guilt he felt, had told him that he couldn't have known, that it wasn't his fault. His XO had told him. Ollie had told him. And now his commanding officer was telling him. He realized that he had no control over the past, but could do something about the future.

Suddenly George stiffened with a new intensity. "Sir, I'll do my best to let it go, and I'll do my best to get back in the saddle and take the fight to the enemy. Trying to help my men will be the best way for me to get some closure as well, I think."

Jordan smiled. "I think you're right, George. You have three more days of leave until you sail again. I thought that you might spend some of that time talking to Captain Warner of the *Sealion*. You may not be aware of it, but *Sealion* hit one of the oil tankers in that convoy you attacked. That tanker spilled oil into the sea, and that oil caught on fire. How many men died in agony in those flames? How many others died because they were coated with that oil? It's impossible to know, George, but Captain Warner has been having nightmares about it, and he has been talking of resigning his commission. I spent over an hour yesterday talking to him about it. I think you both can relate to one another, and I think it would be a good idea for you to spend some time together before you ship out again. Maybe you can encourage each other. War is a hard thing, George. Many are killed, many more are wounded, and as you know, not all of the wounds are physical ones. It's those other wounds that are sometimes more deadly, George, and harder to deal with. I'm proud of you, and proud of your men. Heal up, George, and help others heal. You might just be giving your greatest contribution to our cause by doing so."

George stood to go, shaking hands with Jordan. He was now resolved to obey Jordan's command to heal, and to help others heal. As he left the office he stopped to ask the secretary if she knew how he could contact Captain Warner of the *Sealion*. "I need to take him out to lunch," he said. "We have a lot to talk about."

Chapter 38: The Long View

The bus ride west through the foothills had been a sweet tonic for his soul. The beautiful long grass, the sight of cattle feeding placidly there, the anticipation of home all worked together to bring inner tranquility and a sense that all might be right with the world after all. He had been able to remove the eye patch he had worn for several weeks, and his eye seemed to clear a little bit more every day. The oil had damaged his vision a bit, but he hoped that in time he'd be able to see well enough to shoot down another cougar or bear or elk or wolf. He couldn't wait to join the older men on a hunt through the charming mountains near home. He thought about how he was older now too, not the goofy kid who had gone off to war over three years ago. He had been idealistic then, probably too idealistic. He had been unfamiliar with the world then, unable to comprehend how vast it was, what troubles it contained, what adventures and misadventures were possible. He had gone in as a grunt, a volunteer, a boot. Now he was a veteran. He had killed other men, and he had watched other men die. He had seen too many die, really. Memories of storming the beaches, of the night when the Jap had inadvertently impaled himself on his upraised bayonet, of burying Bennie Friedman, counseling Walter Horn to no avail, memories of Camp Changi and the death of his fellow soldiers building that railway, all the memories muddled together, and he had trouble shaking them out of his mind.

But he was almost home now. The bus had gone through Billings and Livingston and Bozeman, and was now south of Helena pulling into Butte, and was only about an hour from Missoula. He planned to walk home from there. It was several miles, but he had worked himself back into reasonable shape, and he had little to carry. All his belongings had been lost when he was captured, and his duffel bag didn't weigh more than twenty pounds. *I've got to get back into tiptop condition so I can hike the mountains again,* he thought. He was determined to pick up with his life right where he left off. They had told him in his debriefing and discharge that he might have trouble concentrating and with nightmares. He believed it. He had struggled to regain a normal sleeping pattern, and some of the memories were persistent, and not pleasant or welcome.

But he was a tough mountain man after all, named after a legend, and he was set on doing some real living and putting the death and destruction far behind him. The solitude and grandeur of the mountains was as good a place as you could find for doing just that. The bus pulled into Missoula more or less on time, and he got off and took in a deep breath. Nothing like mountain air! The other fellows didn't know what they were missing.

It had been a hard thing to say goodbye to his friends. Their closeness made parting something he dreaded with a passion. But it had to be done. Hack Wilson was on his way to his hometown to start training for that dentist business he was going to start, with *Henry James Wilson, Doctor of Dentistry* on his shingle. Ollie and Virgil were going north to keep a promise before heading back south to their odd vocabulary and their homespun humor. Tank was on his way right now to the Texas plains. Yeah, everybody, including Kit, was going home. They had grown closer than most men would ever be, close as only men in war can be. They had seen too much of life really, too much bloodshed and suffering, enough to last three lifetimes, and they were only in their early twenties. What would it be like to come home again and take up where they left off?

It was impossible in a way. Nobody could go through what they had gone through and ever be normal again. Wives and girlfriends and mothers would never understand, and Dad wouldn't understand either. Some fathers, like Tasker's, had fought in the Great War, and they understood. But Kit's dad hadn't been the right age, had never been in the military, and he wouldn't know what it was like. Trouble was, Kit didn't have a vocabulary that could put it into words, either. The only person Kit knew who could get close would be Herb Johnson, but he was gone. Kit tried to remember that poem about Flanders Fields that Herb had quoted a few times for him while they were at Changi. He'd have to look it up at the library when he had more time and try to memorize it.

Herb. Hack. Tasker. Ollie and Virgil and Tank and Bennie Friedman. What was Danvers' advice? *Make no friends. War is hard enough as it is.* Right. Make no friends. But without friends life really wasn't worth much, was it?

He topped the ridge and looked down on the old home place. And then he looked beyond, at vistas that plainsmen only got to see on rare visits before returning to their dusty homes in the flatlands. The Rocky Mountains! His bad eye was giving him some trouble, but he could still see good enough to appreciate their magnificence. The evergreens were still thick, and rose until they reached the timberline around eleven thousand feet, where snow was accumulating. It might only be September, but up there the snows came early and often. The pebbled mountain path led down towards the house, and he could see three of his younger siblings and his father waving. Dad ran inside the house, and moments later he and Mother came out, clapping their hands for joy as they welcomed home their son.

Chapter 39: Keeping a Promise

The two sailors stopped a passerby and one of them asked, "Can you tell me how to get to Manchester Avenue?" The Bostonian smiled at the Southern drawl, and said "Well, youse oughtta just hail a cabbie. Give him the address and he'll get you dere." The stranger shuffled off again, and the two men shrugged shoulders. One turned to his comrade and said, "I guess we should do that. I don't know what else to do. I can't understand what these people are talking about, and I'm getting a little tired of asking."

The other man immediately took action. "We'll wave down one of these fellas," he said. "We kinda learned to call cabs and find our way around while we were in Pearl before we were sent stateside, and we can do the same thing here." He said this as he stepped to the curb and waved down a Yellow Cab, which swung over to pick up the two servicemen. "Can you take us to thirty-two fifteen Manchester Avenue?" one of the men asked the cabbie. "It's somewhere in Salem."

"Salem?" said the taxi driver. That's twenty-five miles from here. Are you sure youse want me to take youse dat far? It's gonna cost youse."

"Whatever it costs, we've gotta go. We promised a friend we'd take care of something for him."

The cabbie nodded, and they set off. Thirty-five minutes later they arrived at the expensive, stately house on Manchester Avenue in the nicest neighborhood in Salem. The two soldiers weren't exactly sure that it qualified as a mansion, but it sure looked like one to them. They felt poor and were not just a little intimidated by the imposing structure and cultivated grounds, but they were here to do something for a fallen friend, and they meant to get it done. The two went up to the massive front door and rang the doorbell. A chambermaid answered and asked them what their business was. "We've come to see Mr. and Mrs. Johnson. It's about their son Herb. We knew him in the service."

The maid started as though struck by something, and a tear came to her eye. "I'll go get Mrs. Johnson. Please come in and wait in the lobby."

It seemed like a long wait to the two uncomfortable sailors, but within a couple of minutes a beautiful, cultured woman appeared and greeted the two G.I.'s, offering them her hand. "Marian tells me you knew Herbert. Is that true?"

"Yes, ma'am. I'm Virgil Ballard, and this is Ollie Hill. We met Herb at boot camp, and we'd of never made it through without his help. He was a swell man, I can tell ya."

Mrs. Johnson asked the two men to sit down in the visiting room. "Would you like some coffee or tea, or anything? Marian will get it for you."

"No thanks, ma'am," said Ollie. "We just wanted to visit with you awhile and tell you how much we liked your son."

"You are so kind. I'm sorry my husband isn't here, but I'll be sure and tell him of your goodness. What can you tell me about Herbert?"

Virgil responded by saying, "Herb helped us pass our tests so we could get through the naval academy. We wouldn't have made it without him." Ollie joined in, "Herb is the smartest guy I've ever met, and he didn't have to help us, but he did. He never looked down on us because we were dumb Southern boys, and I'll always consider him one of the best friends I ever had."

Virgil ventured to ask Mrs. Johnson a question. "Ma'am, if it isn't prying, are you the one who taught Herb to love poetry so much? Being around him was just like walking into a library. I never saw a man know so many beautiful words from memory. It seemed like he had a poem for everything."

The beautiful mother's eyes got misty at the question, and she looked away for a moment. "I guess you could say that," she whispered. "He was the best son a mother could ask for; so bright and willing to learn. Everyone who knew Herbert believed he showed all the promise in the world. But now that promise will never be fulfilled..." She broke down as she said these last words, and it made for an uncomfortable few moments for all of them. "Please excuse me," she muttered after she had composed herself a bit. "As you can imagine, this is a bit hard for me. But it's also so helpful. I need to talk about him, and I am so happy you've taken the time to stop by. I'll try to keep my emotions in check. Everything you can relate to me about his time in the service is a treasure to me. He wrote often, but of course after he was captured we heard nothing of him until that terrible day when they told us he had perished."

Ollie and Virgil did the best they could to relate to Mrs. Johnson some of the specifics of their time with Herb during training and on board the *Edwards*, especially some of the funny times, and some of the poems he shared. They told her of their times floating on the ocean in rafts, and their capture and imprisonment at Camp Changi, being careful not to share some of the worst details of camp life or the horrors of the *Rakuyo Maru* hold or Herb's last few hours on the raft, where he lost his mind and raved like a lunatic. They did share some of Herb's last moments of lucidity, when, after he had calmed for a bit he told of his love for his parents and for Karen, his girl. They also were quick to point out Herb's responses to their "Thankful Game," and that his parents were always at the top of his thankful list. "He sure loved you and your husband, ma'am," said Ollie. "You couldn't wish for a more grateful son."

Once again Mrs. Johnson's emotions betrayed her, but she gathered herself and said, "We didn't deserve him. His father encouraged him to use his gifts to make a better world. Sounds like he did just that."

Virgil said, "Well, he sure did, ma'am. Everyone who knew Herb was blessed by him. He was a great sailor, a fine friend, and a credit to his country and his family. I'll never forget him."

After their emotional visit, the boys said goodbye, and then talked about Mrs. Johnson most of the way to the bus station. Virgil opened up. "I'm glad we stopped. I think it helped her to talk about Herb. I'm sure she'll tell her husband and Karen too." Ollie responded, "We had to do it, Virg. You remember what we said on the raft after Herb was gone. We wanted to stay alive so we could come and tell Herb's folks what a great guy he was. I think we succeeded. She must have thanked us ten times for coming." Virgil nodded assent, and the two friends moved on to a discussion about their futures.

"I guess you're going back to Alabama, huh Ollie.?"

"Sure. Don't know where else I'd go. Not sure what I'm going to do when I get there. Reckon my cousin still runs a garage, and I'm sure he'll let me work there until I figure something out. What about you, Virg?"

The Okie didn't hesitate. "I've thought a lot about what I can do. I was going to get into the gas business before the war started anyway. They're drillin' wells like crazy back where I'm from, and I know how to work. I figure I can work my way up until I own some of those wells." Virgil said this with a grin, and Ollie knew he'd be alright. After what they'd been through, both of them could probably handle anything this life threw their way. "Just be sure and come see me sometime, old pardner. We've done a heap of livin' together the last couple of years, haven't we? I'd hate to never see you again."

Ollie responded, "Yeah, maybe I'll just take me a trip out west sometime. I ain't never been to Oklahoma before. You sure it's worth a sight-see?"

Virgil answered, "It's got the best people on earth, and some pretty nice countryside too."

"Just remember that the buses and trains run both ways," Ollie finished. "You owe me a trip too, to see my old stompin' grounds."

Ollie's bus left over two hours before Virgil's, but the Oklahoman was there to see his friend off. "I ain't ever gonna forget you, you no-good Alabaman. Take care now, hear. If you know how to write, drop me a line now and again."

Ollie gave Virgil a giant bear hug, and found the words just wouldn't come easy. So much to say, but so little ability to voice it. *Sure could use old Herb and his way with words right now.* "Bye, Virg. I'll be thinkin' of you." The bus pulled away slowly, and the two friends had one more chance to see each other through the window and wave goodbye. It sure was a long two hour wait for Virgil Ballard until his bus came to take him south…and home to the red soil of Oklahoma.

Chapter 40: Home at Long Last

The lone flyboy got off the bus and found a ride with someone heading out toward the family home. *Texans sure are nice,* he thought. *Wish everyone in the world was that way. Probably wouldn't have so many wars.*

It was early September and as usual it was dusty, and hot. The cooler weather usually didn't make an appearance around here until well into October or even November. He could remember a few times as a youngster playing pickup football games on Christmas Day in his shirtsleeves. Panhandle weather. It could do almost anything, and sometimes could do several very different things all in one day. But he loved the place. It was home.

He arrived at the long driveway, thanked the man who drove him, and, shouldering his kit, made his way towards the house. He had called the folks when he arrived in Amarillo, and he knew they would be expecting him. His brother had already come home with several medals, including a Purple Heart. Thankfully Seth's injury wasn't too serious. Tank had his injuries too, injuries from his time building the Railway of Death, injuries sustained from vengeful Korean guards trying to push him into the hold on the transport, and psychological injuries too. He had left home dreaming of flying, and he had learned to pilot the hardest plane the U.S. had to fly. He never lost a man in combat, but lost a host of friends during the rest of his long journey home. He was proud of what he had accomplished, but he hadn't really become a war hero. *How long ago it seemed that he stood in the garden, hoeing away and dreaming of being the next Lindbergh! That was a lifetime ago.*

Tank noticed that his younger brothers were now the caretakers of the garden and fruit trees. They had kept everything up in pretty good shape, too. Dad had made sure they understood his expectations of them fulfilling their duties, finishing their chores. The fruit trees were several feet higher than when he left. He wondered how tall his brothers had also grown, and how lady-like his younger sisters would be by now. It was more than three years since he had left. Mom and Dad have probably grown older too, a lot older worrying about Seth and me. *I am thankful to the Lord for getting us back home again. Not every family can say thank You for that.* He wondered about Herb's family, and Tasker's, and Fred Dixon's, and so many more. He had found out that the men in the second raft, the one headed by Peachy Monroe, the other raft afloat after they ditched his B-24, those men had all survived, been picked up by a troop transport, and they had rejoined the squadron to fly another two dozen missions against the Railway of Death. *To think of it, he was stuck in Changi trying to build it while they were doing their best to bomb it out of existence!* War sure was a funny thing. But he was glad they had made it. That day after the downpour he had wondered about their fate.

Tank remembered the "Thankful Game" they had played on the raft to get their minds off their misery for a time. Virgil had described in delicious detail the chicken-fried steak, mashed potatoes, green beans, homemade rolls, and salad, and had added, "of course no chicken-fried steak dinner was complete without homemade gravy. Lastly they would eat the cherry cobbler. My mother is famous for her cherry cobbler." He smiled and wondered what Mom would have on the stove for their supper. She might not be famous for her cherry cobbler, but she still made a fine one. In fact, he couldn't ever remember eating a bad cobbler.

Tank's family realized he had arrived, and with shouts and squeals and tears they all rushed out of the house and hugged him at once. He winced a bit from the pain of the still-bothersome sores he had received from the guards, but the love and comfort of those hugs made this a small price to pay. Tank, the sturdy boy from the Texas panhandle, who had grown up so far away from airplanes and ships and adventure, now had adventure stories to tell for a lifetime. At long last he was home, ready to begin telling those stories to the ones he loved.